The Art of Action Research in the Classroom

The Art of Action Research in the Classroom

Christine Macintyre

David Fulton Publishers
London

David Fulton Publishers Ltd
Ormond House, 26–27 Boswell Street, London WC1N 3JD
Website: http://www.fultonbooks.co.uk

First published in Great Britain by David Fulton Publishers 2000

British Library Cataloguing in Publication Data
A catalogue record for this book is available from the British Library

ISBN 1–85346–701–4

Typeset by Elite Typesetting Techniques, Eastleigh, Hampshire
Printed and bound in Great Britain by Biddles Ltd, *www.biddles.co.uk*

Contents

Foreword

This sympathetic, highly readable text is designed to help teachers and students to carry out action research. Many will receive from the start of their planning, two conflicting messages – one from what they hear, the other from what they read. One is that teachers are continually engaged in the cyclical processes of planning implementation and evaluation of their classroom work and thus that action research is essentially experience and common sense. The opposite and contrasting view lays great stress on the undoubted complexity and pitfalls of classroom research, to the neglect of its inbuilt and invaluable advantages. These are principally, the opportunity to conduct systematic investigations in a context which is familiar to pupils and intimately understood in all its complexity by their teachers. Secondly, the kinds of research question teachers and students ask are likely to be relevant and meaningful within that context and the answers they obtain will influence their future practice.

The major limitation of research carried out within a particular classroom concerns generalisation beyond it. As Dr Macintyre points out however, the aim is the improvement of learning experiences for a particular group of pupils and 'surely no-one could object to that?'

The book follows the logical sequence of the action research process and throughout emphasises the need for clear thinking and maintaining a focus on the research question. The need to avoid unnecessary deviations is stressed along with a realistic awareness that real classrooms do make demands on staff's flexibility and responsiveness.

The use of illustrative verbatim extracts from students' reports of their own research activity is most effective. They lead the reader easily into complex issues with the colour and conviction of reality. There are several salutary reminders of differing perceptions and interpretations that may readily arise in the various participants and of the need of researchers to be aware of this possibility. One example is of pupils' misleading accounts to their parents of classroom research.

The book addresses a range of ethical questions such as the compliance of young pupils and the danger that this may be taken advantage of. The importance of courtesy, consideration and full communication at all stages of the research is given due prominence.

In conclusion, readers will both enjoy and derive practical and moral support from this concise, clear and thoughtful introduction to action research the classroom.

Dr Judith Watson
Reader in Education,
University of Edinburgh.
April 2000

Acknowledgements

There are many people who have contributed to this book and I should like to thank them all. First, my thanks must go to the many teachers and student teachers who over the years have discussed their research ideas and hopes, their doubts and difficulties, their frustrations and eventually their exhilarations! Nearly all claimed that action research was a worthwhile thing to do because of the insights it provided into their teaching as well as the pupils' learning experiences. As a result of carefully investigating an idea, the teachers claimed that they could understand and therefore explain what made their pupils 'tick'! Sometimes finding out held real surprises; surprises which caused the teachers to re-evaluate their approaches to the curriculum, their pace of interacting, the scope of what was envisaged, even the expectations which could reasonably be held. Without this kind of investigation, these surprises and therefore the opportunities to make positive teaching and learning changes could well have been missed in the comings and goings of the classroom day.

Thank you too, to the children who participated in the research and allowed their responses and reactions to permeate the pages of this book. They were very enthusiastic, usually delighted by their progress and intrigued by the results!

And last, and not least, thank you to Catriona, Richard and Shauna for their patience and forbearance and for the professional presentation of the script.

Introduction

This is an introductory text which explains how to carry out action research in the classroom. It aims to help teachers and student teachers who wish to make changes in their classroom practice, plan, implement and evaluate these procedures according to the principles of action research. This enables them to claim with confidence that they have found why the changes have or have not benefited their teaching and the pupils in their care. And if these teachers are prepared to share their findings, they can take knowledge and understanding about the effects of change forward so that the 'best' education can be obtained for the greatest number of children.

The classroom is a complex social environment with different groups of people from different backgrounds and different levels of experience in adapting to anything new, and so innovations which 'work' in one situation may be of only limited use in another. It is important, therefore, that teachers in many different environments become involved in classroom research, for then they can accumulate a bank of strategies to let others select the ones most likely to be helpful in their own context – thus making generalisation, one of the important aims of action research, a more realistic possibility. Moreover, these teacher-researchers will have evidence to show that they have been innovative and reflective, or that they have kept abreast of current developments and tried them out, or indeed that 'imposed' changes do or do not benefit their children in their classrooms. These are all confidence-giving and status-enhancing moves!

Furthermore, such findings, i.e. those based on evidence, are very important beyond the classroom, for only through being alerted to the advantages and disadvantages of change in different contexts can policy makers make informed decisions as to the best way forward. If they are to do this, they have to be kept informed.

The action research process is one of innovation and careful evaluation. In many ways it is similar to the reflective teacher process which many constantly use to improve or extend their teaching. The difference comes in the application of the principles of action research. When this is done, teachers can move beyond giving descriptions of what occurred to giving explanations of why. And so, on the basis of evidence, they can justify continuing or abandoning the change or they can make adjustments to make it better. Furthermore, they will be enabled to say, not 'I think' or 'I feel', but 'I know.' In this way, 'action research, through developing the "practical wisdom" (Elliot 1991) and "situational understanding" (Elliot 1993a) of the practitioner researcher, constitutes "a powerful means of professional development"' (Somekh 1995). It 'enhances professional competence' (Hopkins 1994).

Action research then, is a recognised and approved way of carrying out self-appraisal through evaluating any or all of the activities which make up classroom practice. It is a disciplined method of investigation which gives credibility to the claims that are made. It is a research method which 'fits' the parameters and ethos of the classroom for it allows teachers and pupils to be active change agents, not simply participant observers (Bryant 1996). This means that teachers are fully involved in conceptualising then implementing changes rather than being observers who do not wish to disturb the scene. This is important, for it means that changes can be planned for specific children in their own context. And so, even experienced teachers can find out things they did not know and children can try new ways of learning. 'Having a go' can lead to discovery, fun and a real sense of achievement, for finding what makes children 'tick' is endlessly intriguing!

But why should teachers need to be action researchers? Surely the complexities of teaching are demanding enough? Is this just an extra burden, for it is time-consuming and really quite difficult to do well, or is it a credible way of evaluating the constant changes which bombard the classroom? Or, on a more personal level, can it improve teaching through encouraging reflection, or contribute to the acquisition of a first or higher degree? It can do all of those things, but only if criteria such as rigour and validity guide the teachers as they plan their action, then gather, analyse and whenever possible publish their findings.

What sorts of things lend themselves to being researched?

There are many important and fascinating topics within the teaching day which are crying out to be investigated in context. Sometimes these arise from innovations 'advised' by the government, e.g. 'whole class teaching to replace ability groups,' 'testing as a means of improving standards,' 'teaching reading through phonics,' 'moving away from a child-centred approach in the Nursery,' 'integrating children with very special needs into the mainstream classroom,' 'team teaching' to name but a few. Sometimes teachers themselves, through careful reflection generate the ideas which they anticipate will close the 'performance gap between their aspirations and their practice' (Ebbutt 1985), or they may wish to extend their teaching by trying something new and so improve the learning experiences of some or all of their pupils, perhaps by 'introducing self-assessment,' 'evaluating children's problem-solving strategies,' 'paired reading,' 'monitoring the impact of having an Urdu-speaking Mum to describe aspects of her culture,' or 'evaluating measures to stop bullying'. Again a long and disparate list.

Sometimes student teachers must carry out small-scale pieces of action research as part of their studies, because universities believe that learning research skills while they are in a supported environment will have significant gains. The first is that the students will learn how to reflect and self-evaluate and so gain confidence in discussing and improving their teaching; the second that they gain a new skill which may enable them to get a post in a school which expects its staff to have some research experience. They may even decide to become full-time researchers!

What sorts of things are these student teachers likely to investigate? Many tutors encourage them to examine an aspect of their developing competence e.g. 'improving questioning', 'using storyboards to help sequencing', 'analysing children's drawings to determine their developmental status', or they may look at an aspect of classroom organisation, e.g. 'comparing children's work when they work in attainment and social groups', 'designing classroom rules', or 'using visual aids (or other resources) in a novel way'. If they do this, then their research 'action plan', (which is really a series of interventions carefully planned to provide evidence to answer their research question), can become part of the teaching forward plan rather than something artificially added on which could disrupt the usual classroom organisation.

There are many choices for both teachers and students and each one is important, for all are likely to mean changes in classroom practice – in what is taught, in the way it is presented, in the underlying management and organisation, in decisions about what the 'intended outcomes' are to be and how they are to be monitored to ensure that the most effective teaching results. No matter the source or the scale, or even the purpose, any kind of change has to be carefully considered, for if it impinges on what the children are to learn or how they are to learn it, then it means taking an important step with possibly long-lasting consequences.

And so teachers contemplating research have to be able to do two things. Firstly, to justify what they are intending to do in terms of their own professionalism, the children's needs and possibly in relation to current educational developments. Secondly, they must anticipate in what ways the envisaged change might improve the status quo, for it goes without saying that any change must be planned to make things better.

The action research method has many benefits and some limitations just as all research methods do. Understanding both the pros and the cons and recognising how they influence the investigation is an important part of being a credible researcher. All of these will be explained in the following chapters as the detail of the method unfolds. The chapters themselves are based on the questions which new researchers have consistently asked. They are answered to help those who want to find out why... The questions are:

1. What is action research? What principles should apply? (Chapter 1)
2. Why has the research to be guided by the literature? What is meant by reading 'critically and analytically'? How do I prepare to write a literature review? (Chapter 2)
3. How do I formulate a clear, concise research question? (Chapter 3). This leads on to the further question: What else do I need to consider before beginning the action? Ethical considerations; Bias; Reliability; Validity; Negotiating access; The context.
4. What is involved in organising an action plan? What data gathering instruments can I use? (Chapter 4)
5. How can I analyse my data and record my findings? (Chapter 5)
6. How do I structure a research report/thesis? (Chapter 6)

This long list is not meant to be off-putting; it is comprehensive and should cover every stage of the action research process. And of course, no-one needs all the information at once. These questions move sequentially through the planning, implementing and evaluating stages of the research.

The first try is often said to be the most difficult but also most rewarding, for there is a special sense of discovery and ownership of a new development. Then there is the pleasure and satisfaction gained from having tackled a difficult process and having positive feedback, as well as lots of clues about how to do it better next time.

CHAPTER 1

Action research explained

This chapter gives an overview to set the scene, then subsequent chapters deal with each issue in a more detailed way. First of all a comprehensive definition:

> Action research is an investigation, where, as a result of rigorous self-appraisal of current practice, the researcher focuses on a 'problem' (or a topic or an issue which needs to be explained), and on the basis of information (about the up-to-date state of the art, about the people who will be involved and about the context), plans, implements, then evaluates an action then draws conclusions on the basis of the findings.
>
> (Macintyre 1991)

This may be summarised as in Figure 1.1

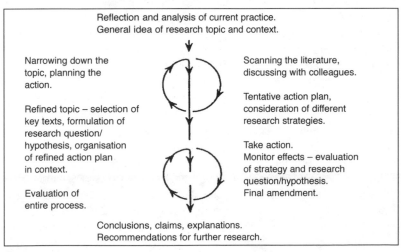

Figure 1.1 An action research cycle

The research must progress steadily through the stages outlined in Figure 1.1 or nothing new would ever be discovered, but all the time as the action unfolds, there is constant reflection on the ongoing process. This comes through discussing with others, constantly reconsidering and evaluating e.g. the advice taken from the literature, the developing research question and all aspects of the action-plan in the light of the ongoing investigation. This means that in reality, the process is cyclical – it is not straightforward at all.

Implicit in the definition and the figure are the principles which must be followed if the investigation is to merit the term 'action research'. The first is that the researcher 'reflects on current practice, and as a result focuses on a "problem" which needs to be explained'. What does this involve?

This may mean re-examining established ways of teaching or classroom procedures, or if there is a gap in present practice, trying something for the first time. It may mean evaluating recommended teaching strategies or different modes of classroom organisation, or experimenting with innovative ways of teaching or taking steps to understand and improve some aspect of the children's development. There are many, many fascinating possibilities, but the chosen one will concern something from the repertoire of teaching competences that requires explaining, hence the non-critical research use of the term, 'problem'.

This could suggest that the research was based on the negative premise of 'having to do something to improve the status quo', but this is not the case. The fact that extremely busy teachers are prepared to go the extra step to ensure that their practice is as good as it can be, is the real thrust behind classroom research. As has been said, the research process begins with reflection, and this can be very difficult, especially for experienced teachers who have built up a repertoire of successful coping strategies. These have been established through much trial and error and selecting the best personal way, and so it is not easy to review that process critically and make decisions about what new things to try. And yet at the same time these teachers would want to disavow any suggestion that they were entrenched in tried and tested ways. Perhaps the 'promise' that trying out new things can re-energise the classroom through bringing a sense of the unknown into play will tempt some who are reluctant? For surely it is these experienced teachers who are the ones who can leave established routines, confident in the knowledge that their teaching will not be threatened? McIntyre (1993) highlights this difficulty, but endorses the value of reflection. He claims that: 'learning (for experienced teachers) is dependent on them examining assumptions and considerations which make sense of their actions as teachers: without reflection they cannot change their practice in a controlled or deliberate way.' This is because so much of their practice is intuitive, i.e. based on long-practised skills. Interestingly, he also explains that reflecting on practice is less difficult for students or inexperienced teachers because in new teaching, 'every halting step is achieved through conscious control'. This being the case, reflection is a constant ongoing process. Students do not have many 'advantages' over experienced teachers. Perhaps this is one?

The next part of the definition, i.e. the one which refers to 'the up-to-date state of the art', is a way of describing the second principle, i.e. 'that both the choice of topic and the way of investigating it, must be informed by recent literature', and here research journals are particularly fruitful sources of information.

Why is the literature so important?

There are several reasons. The first, for those who have difficulty deciding on their topic, is that browsing through the literature can pinpoint a topic which would be both relevant and interesting for the researcher and contextually suitable. Or, by highlighting key words and phrases, the literature can help to focus thinking on particular aspects of a topic and help new researchers realise that a similar investigation could be possible/feasible/realistic in their own context. This can be a great help in getting started.

The next, and this is critically important for all researchers, is that studying and selecting and eventually reporting the literature which has been used, gives the work an academic base. It demonstrates that the researchers have studied developments in the particular field of enquiry and that they will begin their own investigations from an informed stance. This gives everyone confidence, for it shows that what is to be attempted has been carefully considered. Moreover, other researchers may have spent a great deal of time and effort making a similar investigation and it would be inefficient to replicate work when the opportunity is there to extend what has been achieved. In this way new projects can take understanding forward, and this, i.e. 'research extending knowledge' (Brown 1990), is what research is all about.

The extension of knowledge depends on the formulation of the critically important research question which emanates from the guidance offered by the literature, i.e. from the experts in the particular field. Framing this question is not easy, for sometimes different authors have conflicting theories, and the new researcher must compare and contrast and evaluate these ideas, then contextualise i.e. envisage how apt they could be for the new investigation, before deciding on the best way forward. Or perhaps the reported research is based on a large-scale study and only snippets can be of use to researchers based in one classroom. And so decisions need to be made as to the most appropriate ways to design the action plan and gather the data. These will be important in ongoing and final evaluations when the researchers will ponder questions such as, 'Was that the best strategy for my children in my classroom?', and 'Did the literature that I selected give me the most helpful advice?'

Another important reason for being guided by the literature is that it can alert readers to potential research difficulties. Quite often, researchers can have really interesting ideas, but not until they go to the literature do they realise the scale and complexity of their envisaged change. This is particularly true if the topic is something like 'raising the self-concept of pupils' – a topic which has great appeal for students. Of course this is a laudable thing to attempt, but the literature shows how difficult it is, and how the students, in their short time with the children, could hardly begin to influence other 'impinging variables' or in non-research language, influences outside the school over which they have no control but which severely affect the self-concept of their children. In alerting readers to the complexities of their chosen topic, the literature shows how important it is to consider the parameters of the investigation in relation to outside influences and the time-scale available.

Certainly those who intend to write up their research as a thesis must ensure that their topic is not ad hoc, but can be supported by other investigations in the field, for these will have to be carefully selected and critically analysed to show how they have informed the subsequent investigation.

Then the definition asks researchers to consider, 'the people who will be involved, and the context', in other words the participants and the place where the investigation will happen. Those who carry out the research have the responsibility of working with children in school who are, to some extent, a captive audience with little power to say 'no'. And so, all of the time, throughout the preparation and implementation stages, the researchers must consider the suitability of their chosen topic for the children in terms of their age, their stage of development, their attainment, their personalities and possibly their friendship groups. They must also monitor the ongoing process carefully to detect any negative effect.

Their next task is to consider their specific research environment, e.g. the availability of others to help make observations and so reduce bias, the 'paper, pen, tape recorder, and hall time' kind of resources, the amount of time that will be available, whether the children have recently encountered change and how they reacted to it, the social factors inside and even outside school, in other words all the contextual factors which could impinge on the children's participation and thus influence the results.

The next part of the definition claims that the researchers must 'plan, implement then evaluate their action'. The plan is designed to answer a clear, concise, unambiguous and genuine research question. Once this has been formulated, and this takes some time because it has to be suitable, not just for the research topic in the abstract, but for the topic in the context where the research will be carried out, the teachers themselves can design and carry out a series of actions i.e. an action plan, which will produce evidence, i.e. research data, to answer it.

How will the data be gathered?

The action plan provides the opportunities to gather data about certain categories of response – as opposed to everything which happened. This is the evidence which will answer the research question. To do this effectively, different data gathering methods must be planned ahead of the first action and ideally administered by different people, so that the findings may be compared and 'true' results recorded. This is called triangulation. Each record, whether it be taking field notes or completing observation schedules or tape recording oral contributions to a discussion, should be unobtrusive, otherwise the children will change how they behave and distort the data. Furthermore, the aim is to gather objective evidence of things which consistently occur, rather than 'one-off atypical blips' which could distort the findings. This means that data has to be gathered on several occasions and possibly in different venues to try to obtain a 'usual' picture of events.

Collecting objective evidence is not easy, and one reason is that the researchers know their subjects so well. This is at once a strength and a weakness of the action research method. There is no doubt that teachers, knowing their own practice and their pupils intimately, can formulate the most useful and relevant research questions for their particular context. In addition, they are experienced observers of children of that particular age group and understand the nuances and foibles that occur. These are clearly strengths. But unless care is taken, they could be weaknesses too. This is because such familiarity can prevent teachers seeing 'clearly', as possibly a stranger would, for teachers in their own classroom are likely to have preconceived assumptions about their children and how they might cope with any innovation, and may have difficulty seeing beyond these! This is a possible source of bias and can distort the research findings.

5

Therefore another very important principle is that researchers take every possible step to reduce bias and make their findings as objective as possible. If this happens, the research should be as 'reliable' as it can be. This means that if someone else was to carry out the same procedures, then the results would be the same. If anyone thinks this is easy, try asking two people to observe the same part of a lesson and at the end to compare their findings. I guarantee you will be surprised! This kind of mini-activity brings home the pitfalls of teacher research and helps us understand why this method can be justly criticised if the researchers cannot show that they have adhered strictly to the principles which have been established to give the investigation credibility.

If all of this seems too complex, it can be a comfort to realise that carrying out research need not be an individual effort. Groups of teachers can agree a topic and enrich the investigation by having several readers, planners and discussants. Several banks of experience can really illuminate the starting point, e.g. in finding how different teachers cope with unruly behaviour, in collating views on how different teaching methods affect children's learning, or how visual aids have been used to reinforce problem-solving strategies. Certainly there will be more eyes to reduce bias, perhaps through taking quite simple measures like changing groups at the observation and data collection times.

A cooperative arrangement like this will mean that more children can be studied and so more data will be available for analysis. In addition, the findings might point to explanations of how and why a particular innovation 'worked' in one situation and not in another, thus producing a richer report and possibly helping more teachers understand how the innovation could work for them. This would enlarge the potential generalisation of the research, i.e. the possibility that the findings could be applicable in more 'other' situations. This is very important, for small-scale action research in classrooms can be criticised if the findings are so specific that they are no use to anyone else, i.e. if they are not generalisable (Brown 1990). And several researchers investigating the same topic would hopefully be able to make a significant impact on present understandings and this would be very helpful to the profession. But of course they would have to spend a great deal of time together, deliberating the ideas and action plans and engaging in constant evaluation. Not always an easy thing to do!

N.B. Students who wish to engage in collaborative research for an award, need to check the regulations on this in their own institution and if this is agreed, be sure they are clear on the marking procedures.

The research itself is a lengthy process and researchers eat, live and sleep it. It needs a great deal of commitment. This is why teachers have to be sure that their topic is stimulating and 'enduring' and has enough substance to be worth all the effort. Furthermore, action research isn't simply planning a change and carrying it out. All the time, ongoing evaluations cause amendments, perhaps a shift in strategy, or taking more time, or working with more children, or perhaps redefining the research question itself. There are 'highs and lows', and often researchers feel that it is all too much. But one of the greatest strengths of action research is being able to choose a relevant, timely topic, and another is the facility to react to the context and the findings as they unfold. This does not imply that topics can just be abandoned without careful consideration; it means that as the investigation develops, and other things become significant, there is room to react to surprises and find out even more interesting things. Then it becomes a great thing to have done.

Action research in classrooms then, can be:

- creative;
- contextualised;
- realistic;
- flexible;
- rigorous;
- illuminating.

It is:

- creative, because teachers themselves can choose a topic which is intriguing and challenging as well as being appropriate for the pupils who are involved;
- contextualised, because the entire plan is thought through by teachers in their own setting i.e. people who know the day-to-day planning, the pupils who are to be involved and the classroom organisation which exists. As a result, the action can be meaningful, and be absorbed into the daily routine without disrupting the curriculum;
- realistic, because their intimate knowledge of the context allows teachers to gauge what needs to be done, and what can be done amidst all the other pressures of the classroom day. A small-scale study can give rich findings. Using a sledgehammer to crack a nut is definitely not part of action research;
- flexible, because it can respond to unforeseen circumstances. Very often action research is planned to happen at a certain time each week, but if other contingencies arise, such as pupils being absent or rooms or equipment not being available, then it can be moved. In fact, moving it may be one way of reducing bias. If, for example, the pupils are tired and restless at one particular time of the day, the teachers could attribute their lack of attention to lack of interest in the activity, rather than the tiredness itself. Of course, altering the

schedule would depend on other factors, e.g. whether teachers or pupils from other classes or any outside agencies were involved. These considerations aside, a measure of flexibility is generally possible and this can be important in reducing bias for the findings and preventing stress for the researchers;

- rigorous, because if all the results of the research are to stand scrutiny, i.e. to be reliable and valid, then all the stages have to be carried out according to the principles of action research;
- illuminating, because if these principles are adhered to, the researchers can go beyond describing what occurred and explain why things are as they are. Just unlocking one key or discovering one nugget, rather than a gold mine, can be tremendously revealing and exciting and make all the hard work worthwhile.

Another point concerns originality. Postgraduate research students are often puzzled by the requirement for 'original work' for an M.Ed. or Ph.D. thesis and are nervous of choosing something that has been researched before. It is very difficult, however, to find a truly 'original' topic, but the originality can come from the method, from the different focus which is implicit in the research question, from the context where the action happens, or from the action plan itself as well as from reporting the 'original' responses of the group being studied. It need not mean that a pristine, untouched topic has to be conceptualised.

Let's summarise these principles or 'rules' now and then we'll look at how they can be applied:

- Choose a topic that is relevant and important for you in your context, remembering that your aim is to extend understanding.
- Check that there is enough recent quality literature to give guidance.
- Formulate a clear, concise and genuine research question, and form categories for data collection.
- Plan a series of actions specifically to investigate that question.
- Discover all sources of potential bias and take measures to reduce them.
- Carefully consider the action plan in context, and the effect change could have.
- Analyse the findings, and in the light of what has been discovered, evaluate each stage of the process.

And finally,

- Consider the next step...

Example. Topic: Giving children choices. Researcher: Fiona
Fiona, a 4th year B.Ed.(Hons) student, is reporting back to other students in her year. This was her first experience of action research. As you 'listen', try to identify how the principles of action research guided her planning, her implementation and her evaluation.

She explains:

I chose to have eleven-year-olds for my final placement and found I had thirty-three boys and girls in a state school. There was a nice mix of children from different types of housing around the school and my first impression was that although they were noisy, they were friendly towards each other and to the staff. These children appeared to enjoy being at school. Most of them said they had easy access to the local library which had several computers, so they had resources beyond what the school could provide. This had a significant impact on what I chose to investigate.

Throughout my time at University, I had been intrigued by the idea of 'making children responsible for their own learning'. Everyone at the University implied that this was a good thing, but I hadn't seen much evidence of it on placement. In fact, as the children got older, opportunities for them to be responsible seemed to decrease. Nursery children and infants who had the integrated day kind of organisation could make choices, even if it was only choosing the order of completing their tasks, but after that the timetables were pretty rigid, perhaps because of specialists having to have the classes at certain times. For whatever reason, there wasn't much choice built into the day. This was why I hoped that this would be an interesting and challenging development for my own teaching.

And so I hoped that I would be allowed to try 'giving children choices' as my research topic. I approached the teacher with some trepidation but she was really interested and promised that I could devote Friday afternoons to this, 'when all the work for the week was over'. At first I was a bit put out by that response and wondered if the timing would influence the children's efforts, for Friday afternoons are not the most stimulating times, but then I thought 'Well if it works, then it will show that it is a worthwhile thing to do, and at least I have allocated time.' I knew that this was essential if I was to plan ahead and make decisions about the number and kinds of interactions I hoped to have.

9

Giving them choices seemed a good idea in theory, but once I was committed to trying, I became really worried about how the children would react. Would they cooperate or would they think up all sorts of ideas that I couldn't handle? I was terrified they'd choose sex education. However I decided to give them a free choice because I couldn't talk about freedom and then impose my own ideas. My first reading was Richard Caseby's (1990) paper, which claimed that 'Children are much more grown up than we think', and at that point I nearly abandoned ship! I began to doubt whether I would be able to cope if they selected 'adult' topics. However, to offset that, I discovered that the pupils had just had a lengthy input on sex education, so if it came up as a choice, I could legitimately say that it had been covered already and that was a huge relief. But it made me think much more about the pitfalls of what I was trying to do!

I did two whole weeks teaching before embarking on my research, because I needed to get to know the children, so that in open discussions I didn't say any hurtful things. One child's Gran had just died and perhaps the children would want to talk about death. I had to think how I would approach that. I also needed to build a positive relationship with the pupils so that I could admit at discussion time that I didn't have all the answers to their questions, and that they would have to be the ones that found them out. I felt that if I had some successful teaching under my belt, they'd be less likely to scoff. Also the children had to be confident that I would respect their choices and their contributions, and must not be afraid to say they didn't know. In fact I would have liked longer before starting the research, but I only had a limited time in school.

During these first two weeks I worked on my action plan. I knew I had eight Friday afternoons from 1 p.m. to 3 p.m. and reckoned I could divide the children into groups of four or five. They tended to go around in groups like that and I thought social grouping would be best so that was one organisational problem solved – or so I thought! I was also trying to come up with a focused research question. My early thoughts were, 'What will eleven-year-olds choose to discuss?' but that could be answered by giving a list and didn't look at my teaching or the contributions the children would make. I had to justify why I wanted to introduce choices and consider how my own teaching would improve and what the children would gain. I also had to think about how the data would be collected and my first plan was to tape-record and later transcribe the children's contributions to the discussions while they were in their groups. This would let me identify individual contributions and find what use the innovation had been to individual children.

I hoped the free choice would encourage them to complete a useful investigation that would fulfil the requirements of 'enquiry learning' and that in 'contributing to a discussion' they would develop oral reporting skills. This would allow them to share their new learning without the stress of having to write it down. The children had been doing quite a bit of oral reporting in class and so I hoped that they would be able to cope, especially as it was in groups. Finding this out was part of the contextualisation process.

As a result of much deliberation and consultation with the teacher and my tutor, I eventually refined my research question to, 'If I give children freedom to choose, to what extent will this encourage them to complete a useful investigation and be able to report their findings to their peers?' I hoped that answering this question, which was about evaluating my participation as well as theirs, would lead to a balanced report. I intended to monitor 'being able to choose, keeping on task, and ability to report back' as my categories for gathering evidence.

On the Wednesday of the first research week I explained to the children that in two days they could write anonymous lists of ideas that they would like to discuss or learn more about. Next time I wouldn't do that as they immediately started calling out smutty topics and I had to quell the noise. I hated taking the dominant role I wanted to forgo, but I had to tell them to 'be sensible' and I felt I had already suggested that they should choose 'appropriate' ideas. I hoped the intervening days would eliminate this bias.

On the Friday, I anticipated that since they had had notice of the activity, collecting in anonymous lists of their choices would be quite straightforward and I would have gathered my first lot of data. No joy – because several children were reluctant to write anything, I had to resort to putting suggestions on the board as the children called them out. They then were individually asked to select and write the ones which appealed most, and after collating the ideas we had a fair consensus. The topics were, 'Bullying and what schools were doing to stop it', 'Using drugs and why not?' 'Helping people with disabilities', and 'Fashion trends and make up'. One or two children were disgruntled by this and they were allowed to choose outside the list. By this time I wondered if I'd ever get the investigation off the ground as deciding on the topics had taken a whole day!

However, once the topics were agreed and the children were allowed to choose which one they wanted to investigate, they began to get very enthusiastic. Each group was asked to think of leading a discussion and the important points were put on posters and put up for other classes to see. My data gathering noted all of this. I kept a diary of field notes noting individual comments, and I compiled several observation schedules which noted the contributions made by individual members of the group. As I was doing this I also prepared a 'smiley face questionnaire' to distribute at the end so that the children, again anonymously, could tell me what they thought of this kind of activity. I had hoped to record some of the ongoing group discussions as evidence, but background noise made transcribing the tape-recordings very difficult. At the end, other teachers who had helped with the observation schedules came in to hear the discussions and they, knowing the children, were able to tell me about the quality of individual contributions.

My first overview and evaluation was that all of the children had found out some new things. Thirty had tried to collate information at home although this dwindled over the weeks. Two groups kept wanting to change their topic and never really got going, which was disappointing, but three groups of four were totally enthusiastic. The children's final comments ranged from 'I didn't like it, you should tell us what to do,' to 'It was great – the best thing ever.' I did feel that making the posters for the other children to see kept them interested. This wasn't part of my original plan, so it maybe biased the results? Also the other teachers who had volunteered to observe and help reduce bias couldn't always be free. I just had to report these limitations.

I also realised that not all the children had been able to choose. Calling out the suggestions meant that only the dominant ones got their choice. This was a huge blow; I couldn't think how it had taken so long for me to realise that. I think having to get the research completed meant that I was always planning ahead. Anyway it was too painful to look back. At the end I was exhausted. It's much easier to know in advance what the afternoon will hold, but I felt I had learned such a lot about handing over responsibility and I knew the pupils so much better because they asked so many interesting questions and were prepared to accept that I didn't know the answers. They interacted in a more mature way and were pleased when the other classes wanted to know all about their afternoons. And so, when I came to answer my research question, I could say, 'yes' for most of the group but more individual choice would need to be built in and more commitment shown before I could claim that all the children had been 'active enquiry learners'.

Fiona's final comment was that reading books about research just wasn't enough. 'You have to try it. Sometimes you feel really confident and then like a cold douche you realise you've practically invalidated the whole thing, and you think, "Never again!"' She concluded that she had achieved a lot, but that 'I couldn't really expect to get it all right the first time, but I'll try again a bit – no, much later!'

As you followed Fiona's research steps, you will have realised that she had many things to consider. Let's take a moment to reflect on what she chose to do.

She had no difficulty in choosing a topic for her research, because 'giving children choices' was something she thought would extend her teaching. She anticipated, and this was reinforced by the literature, that the children would take this responsibility seriously and keep 'on task'. However, she had to contextualise quickly, to find if this was something new for her particular school, and if it was, would she be allowed to introduce such an innovation? This agreed, she then had to discover whether it was realistic to ask the children to find out things on their own, i.e. would they have easy access to the kinds of resources which would allow them to find out about their chosen discussion topics in their own time? She couldn't take for granted that the children would be either willing or able. She then had to clarify her research question, which after much thought became: 'If I give children freedom to choose, to what extent will this encourage them to complete a useful investigation and be able to report their findings to their peers?'

By phrasing the question in this way, she could describe and later evaluate her part in promoting the innovation; by asking 'to what extent', she was leaving room for reporting the pros and cons of each group's participation, and by setting up a final outcome, i.e. reporting back, she had an opportunity to gather summative evidence as to whether the innovation had produced something informative and interesting.

Fiona had some difficulty finding helpful literature, and discovered that the readings which were most informative on the children's choices were in the Health Education Section in the library. She also consulted documentation on 'using resources', and on 'positive behaviour management', but actually found that the topics kept most of the pupils absorbed, and that discussing and saying that they had helped her discover things she did not know, was actually motivating for them.

The next stage was to organise her action plan. To some extent this was out of her hands because she was constrained to having two hours on Friday afternoons, but she had to decide if and how she would interact with each group and how and when she would gather data. As she was anxious to record the quality of the process in terms of the contributions made by individual pupils, she devised and completed observation schedules as the children worked. She also noted children's ongoing comments and questions in the form of a diary and this she found invaluable in keeping her own written report 'alive' because she was able to quote verbatim, the things the children found 'amazing' or 'boring' as they carried out their task.

In her research question were several implicit hypotheses which identified categories for her data analysis. These were:

- that P7 children would be able to choose interesting and relevant (to them) topics; (the data would be gathered by anonymous lists);
- that the freedom to choose would keep the children 'on task'; (the data would be gathered by observation schedules filled in by herself and different teacher-observers);
- that having social groups would facilitate harmonious working relationships; (the data would be gathered by field notes and the children's evaluations of the process);
- that the group would be able to lead a discussion based on their findings; (the data would consist of tape recordings of the discussions);
- that the children would evaluate the innovation positively; (the data would be gathered by cartoon questionnaires).

Fiona spoke of her relief at having abandoned her original plan to use video. Although this had seemed a good idea in the early planning stages, in that she had thought it would provide objective evidence, she now recognised and wished to avoid the procedural bias (see p.48) which could result from introducing video in such a short series of interactions.

As you can see, her investigation was based on her making many decisions. What more did she need to know and how would others evaluate this first try? Read on to find out more...

CHAPTER 2

The role of the literature

One of the important principles of action research is that the action plan is informed by the literature, and to meet this criterion, researchers aim to show how a critical and analytic study of (usually) recent literature has informed their research question and subsequent research action. But why? Why not just pick a topic and have a go? Bell (1993) gives a thought-provoking reason why. She explains that, 'Action researchers who read are enriching their experience… and those who don't, will inevitably engage in unproductive reinventing of the wheel.'

Let's consider what this enrichment entails. Certainly it means that those who read will discover what has already been studied in their field of enquiry, and if they go to research journals, it is likely that they will discover the rationale, i.e. why the study was considered important in the first place, the particular aspect that was studied, the method that was selected, the context i.e. where the research was carried out and the people who were involved. All this as well as the findings, i.e. what was discovered. In this way, new researchers can plan their own study enlightened by what has gone before and secure in the knowledge that their new venture has substance and that their findings will take understanding forward.

All of this sounds reasonably straightforward but readers will also find that different authors have different perspectives on the same topic and that these give seemingly conflicting results. This is fascinating, but it can also be confusing until the reader comes to understand the source and the implications of these inconsistencies.

Perhaps the different authors are coming from their own specialist field, e.g. physiotherapists studying children with dyspraxia may be mainly concerned with strengthening specific muscle groups while teachers may work on 'coping in the classroom' skills; perhaps different age groups were studied and this affected what the participants were able to do; perhaps one study lasted for a considerable time *in situ*, gathering qualitative data, i.e. an action research case study, while another studied the responses of large groups by questionnaire, i.e. a survey, and so reported quantitive results. Perhaps the methods were the same but different themes were important, e.g. two teachers might choose to study children's expressiveness in dance, but while one was concentrating on the movement aspect in the hall, the other might be investigating whether there was any transfer of learning between the dance and imaginative writing in the classroom. And so, because different questions were asked, different answers were obtained. And yet the titles and some of the key words in the different studies might have been the same.

All of these aspects need to be understood before the research can be fully appreciated in context and before the research findings can be compared and contrasted in any meaningful way. Only when this is done can gaps in the knowledge base be identified and from these gaps the new research questions can emerge. In effect the researcher is saying, 'From reading (the chosen pieces of work) I have discovered (the complementary and contrasting findings). I have considered how these will influence my own study, and so I will now investigate (an aspect of the gap that has to be filled).'

Students are often concerned when they know they have to read 'analytically and critically' because they are unsure what this means. One way to ensure that reading research meets these criteria is to have a number of questions prepared before beginning to read each text (probably a selection of those listed) and then to compare, contrast and evaluate the relevant answers. Such questions might be:
- What was the research topic?
- What was the main theme?
- What background reading informed the study?
- What was the researcher trying to find out?
- What kind of study was it?
- How many people were involved?
- Where was the study carried out?
- What was the time scale?
- Was the participants' age/social background/willingness to be involved, important?
- How many 'action sessions' were there?
- What data gathering strategies were used?
- What attempts were made to reduce bias?
- What evidence was collected?
- What were the claims that were made?
and very importantly,

- Were the researchers justified in making these claims on the basis of what they had found, i.e. were the claims valid?

A penultimate question which can help new researchers is:

- What did the researchers recommend as the next step?

and finally:

- What does this mean for my study?

This list may appear formidable but these questions can be answered as the reading unfolds and some of the answers can be brief. And if readers take notes as the reading proceeds, then they have evidence of 'critical and analytic' reading which will give a sound basis to their own research and contribute to a substantial Review of Literature chapter in their final thesis.

How to begin

Reviewing the literature. Stage 1: Scanning the field

At the start, some potential researchers, particularly student teachers, may have difficulty deciding on their research topic because, 'there are just so many things I'd like to find out about' or, 'I can't think of anything interesting at all!' In my view the best advice for this second group is to look back at their teaching assessments and find an area which they could usefully work on, because schools will expect them to practise recognised teaching competences such as explaining or managing resources or developing discussion skills. These can be focused to form sound pieces of research. (see p.37). And if that doesn't appeal, a good idea is to browse through a selection of texts on an area of particular interest, because often key phrases can spark off ideas.

Most new researchers however, know the area they wish to investigate. They have a 'felt need to initiate change' (Elliot 1991). This is because they have reflected on their current practice and selected an area that they would like to improve, or they have decided that it would be beneficial for both their teaching and the children if they were to try some current innovation. They realise too, that 'their findings will feedback directly into their practice' (Somekh 1995) and so the work will be worthwhile.

Once the topic is chosen, the first stage is scanning different kinds of literature to find what has been documented in the last ten or so years. Unless this is a historical study, looking perhaps at change in the classroom and how today's youngsters would cope with yesterday's learning scenarios, or a study which wishes to compare today's major theorists with the masters of the past, it is probably best to stay with recent texts. This is because newer research techniques will have informed the findings, and children 'then' will be more like children 'now'. There are likely to be quite a number of readily available texts which suit, although some will approach the topic from a different perspective. This being so, it is best to take some time to sift and select and borrow or buy only those which are the most accessible and which are most relevant to the enquiry. This is much better than buying expensive books hoping that somehow – or anyhow – they will provide the right kind of information!

If finding enough literature is a problem, it can be a good idea to try to focus on the topic and identify the key words which will lead to a successful search.

Example. Topic: Perception and learning. Researcher: Bryony
Bryony thought she would like to study the use of visual aids in the classroom, but when she searched using the key word 'resources', the literature offered little help. And so she began to ponder on what had given her the idea in the first place. It had been a saying, 'To hear is to forget, to see is to understand, but to do is to remember.' When she identified these key terms, i.e. 'hearing,' 'seeing' and 'doing,' she realised that what she really wanted to investigate was perception, i.e. how children's preferred modes of perception affected their learning. There was a wealth of literature on perception and learning, and her visual aids became part of the discovery process to find how children with different ways of learning interacted with these resources. Her vitality and enthusiasm returned.

At the start of any literature search, it is always useful to enlist the help of librarians, for their wide knowledge of texts and where they may be found can be so helpful. They can even help make electronic searches, set up inter-library loans or help identify websites. These can save time in collecting or sending for documentation from research bases within universities. The Scottish Council for Research in Education (S.C.R.E.) in Edinburgh, as one example, provides lists of 'Spotlights' i.e. short research papers which may be downloaded from their S.C.R.E. website at http://www.scre.ac.uk and these are very helpful. They also provide lists of titles and these can give pause for thought; however the range is wide, crossing the whole spectrum of education, and so not all are applicable to individual classrooms or schools.

Electronic databases of journal articles such as ERIC and the British Education Index are rich sources of inspiration and information and it is important that researchers learn to use them. Databases such as ERIC are on the Internet and publishers are increasingly putting journals on-line, so useful resources are increasingly available in different forms.

In any text, the subject index is a good place to begin. It gives instant guidance as to the whereabouts of the topic within the book, and seeing how it appears in different contexts can be enlightening, perhaps even suggesting an alternative focus for the new study.

Example. Topic: Positive interaction. Researcher: Graeme
Graeme reports on how focusing helped him. He explains:

When I began thinking about what would help in my classroom, I decided to study motivation. This was because I knew I had several pupils in my middle ability group who were just doing the minimum amount of work. Someone suggested that David Child's (1986) Psychology and the Teacher (4th ed.) had a readable chapter on motivation, although I was surprised that this topic didn't feature in more recent texts. Anyway, I was lucky enough to find a copy in the library. I went to the index first, 'as instructed!' And when I was browsing through, I came across the topic 'teacher expectations' and how raising these could improve the children's performance. I knew immediately that this was what I really wanted to do, and concentrated on finding readings in that. I was much happier with the notion of trying to change my own style of interaction in the classroom than offering rewards or threatening the kids with dire consequences if they didn't behave. I knew that wouldn't work!

And so I told the children that I was setting out really interesting, but difficult work and explained that this was because I knew they could achieve a very high standard. And all the time I would say things like, 'this is amazing'. Often I felt I was over-egging the pudding but the children just seemed to thrive on the harder work and on the praise which followed their efforts.

Going to the index had not only helped Graeme focus on a more gripping topic, but reading the text gave him ideas on planning the change. He tried to keep his 'high expectations' going across the curriculum but for his research project monitored the pupils' responses, in terms of their 'time on task' and by the quality of their completed work, only in environmental studies. Graeme's class teacher observed his use of the prepared 'higher expectation' inputs so that any claims he later made concerning their effectiveness were valid. This was manageable in the seven weeks he had in school and gave results that encouraged him to continue this successful new approach in subsequent placements and in other areas of the curriculum. He also was confident that this change would help others and so he reported these findings to two cohorts of student teachers about to go on placement, as well as compiling his thesis.

The literature then, can:
- show what has already been done in the particular area;
- identify gaps which would be useful to fill;
- show that an idea is sound;
- provide starter points for new research;
- make suggestions for planning the action;
- justify the suitability of the topic for the particular group of pupils;
- give the researcher confidence that the topic is worth investigating and that the potential for discovering something worthwhile is there.

Stage 2: Selecting key texts

Once the topic has been chosen, a smaller number of key texts, including articles or papers which report research, can be selected. If this is an undergraduate piece of work, perhaps as few as five or six on the same theme can give enough information, in telling what other researchers have studied, what questions they asked, what arguments they put forward, what methods of investigation they used, what they discovered, and what gaps they left behind. The important thing is to read these texts critically (see p.16). Postgraduate work will need a much more extensive foray, but the search will be based on the same process of critical and analytic reading.

As the research topic gradually crystallises, it can be helpful to approach the literature with a number of questions which will show how different authors defined their topic, the investigative strategies they used, what they found and what their recommendations for future investigations were. The answers can help to structure the literature review which forms a central part of any thesis. Some examples from teachers who found this process helpful are now given.

Topic: Reading mathematics
- How important is reading ability in Stage 4 mathematics?
- What concepts cause particular difficulties?
- What kinds of examples/learning activities can best be used to explain these?

Topic: Helping children with movement difficulties
- What is dyspraxia?
- Will maturation help, or is intervention required?
- Are there specially designed intervention programmes?
- What resources and teaching strategies can help these children?

Topic: Drug abuse
- What are the parameters which distinguish between use, misuse and abuse of drugs?
- Are certain groups of pupils more likely to use drugs?
- What kind of teaching input have others found helpful?
- Can schools claim that health education programmes have been effective?

Topic: Encouraging children's talk through drama
- What constitutes drama in the Infant classroom?
- Why should children be reluctant talkers?
- What strategies within drama have been tried to encourage talk?

Topic: Collaborative group work in science
- What is the difference between collaborative and cooperative group work?
- What kind of organisation in science can make this happen?
- In what ways do the learning experiences of the pupils change?

Topic: Making friends
- When do children begin to make friends?
- What do they see as the characteristics of a good friend?
- Why are some children excluded?
- What can teachers do to help?

N.B. These 'going to the literature questions' are not research questions per se. This is because they look back over work that has been completed, whereas research questions are 'genuine enquiry questions' which look forward into the new investigation. Your aim at this stage is to be clear about what it is you want to find out, to have identified several texts intimately concerned with your topic and to formulate questions to structure your reading and note-taking.

The information which comes from your reading is the foundation of both your research question and the action plan, which is the means by which you collect data to answer your research question.

Can you begin to see the logic of the research story?

Taking notes in preparation for writing the review

As you read and prepare to write your literature review, it is essential to keep detailed notes of what you found, where you found it and how each reading might relate to your own research. Even if some seem to have little relevance for your own investigation at that particular moment in time, taking a moment to jot the author's theme, the key concepts or issues which are covered, and the most important findings could prove beneficial later if your study takes an unexpected turn, or when you wish to discuss conflicting perspectives in your review.

The discipline imposed by making notes has another, perhaps less obvious benefit. This is keeping you on track and not letting you stray from your focus. The time for prevaricating, i.e. thinking 'I could do that instead,' is past. Once the topic has been chosen, it is best not to be sidetracked or confusion can easily set in. And so, as you read, avoid being tempted to carry on without recording details of what you discovered. You think you won't forget. Even after several texts on the same theme? I wonder!

Careful and accurate note-taking is really important because one of the most frustrating things about doing research is trying to find a lost 'original source'. You can remember the author's idea, the exact phrases spill tantalisingly through your mind, but where is it exactly? You suspect it is in such and such a book, or journal, but you may be mistaken, or horror of horrors, someone else has the text on extended loan! This can be very bad news, for you can't use someone else's work without acknowledging the original source. If this happens to you – and unless you are meticulously careful it will – you will be very annoyed and distressed that you didn't write it down.

In my experience, the most efficient way to keep records is to use a box of index cards. Of course there are newer, electronic means of storing data and some of these will even cross-reference texts, but these cards can be slipped into a pocket for a library visit and notes can be easily jotted down. Furthermore, they are always just to hand if you need a quick reminder; they can be set out on any table for a recall or cross-referencing session, and the alphabetical ordering is useful in that it simplifies writing the bibliography. (See Figure 2.1.)

The amount of detail which should be recorded on each card can vary with the relevance of the reading to the topic, but enough information is needed to cover inserting the work into the text and into the bibliography. A difficulty arises here. This is that different institutions and publishers vary in how they wish this information recorded. The best idea is to check and then do all the recording in that format. This saves time in altering the

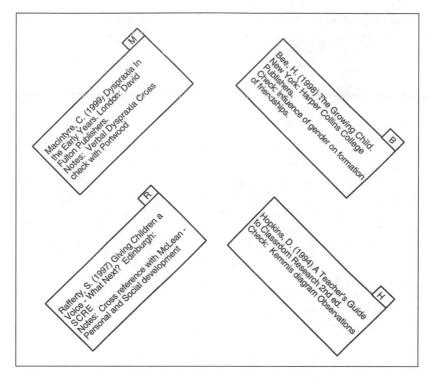

Figure 2.1 Using index cards

layout for inclusion in the review of literature and the bibliography. One usual way is shown here, and more detail can be found on (p.28)

In the text itself, the reference might appear as: 'Bell (1993) advises that "Finding information again some time later is very difficult" and that "methods of recording should be thorough and systematic."' The detail here gives the author's surname and then the date of publication. Thereafter, the actual quoted words are enclosed by quotation marks. Some universities require longer quotes to be indented and italicised, and page numbers to be included in the text.

The insertion in the bibliography would be:

Bell, J. (1993) *Doing your Research Project. A Guide for First Time Researchers in Education and Social Science.* Buckingham: Open University Press.

Here the author's initial comes after the surname, and the date of publication is followed by the title of the book which is italicised. The place of publication is followed by the publisher's name.

Getting it right can be tricky. A helpful hint is to remember that the purpose of the bibliography is to show which texts have been consulted *and* to allow the reader to find the source material quickly. Identifying the source by quote marks or italics lets this happen.

When does the reading happen?

In some brief investigations most of the reading can be done at an early stage, and then be put aside until the 'writing up the thesis' stage when the usefulness of the guidance given by the literature will form part of the evaluation. But in most studies, the reading needs to follow the development of the research question, and so needs to be constantly at hand. This is especially important in action research because the research question may be elaborated or amended as the research continues. In that case continuous guidance from the literature may be required.

As you read, it is useful to note the style of reading which was most informative for you. Were research terms clearly explained? Was the text reader-friendly, giving interesting and relevant examples to clarify or illustrate what was said? If this was helpful, it might be possible to echo that kind of approach in your own thesis.

Considering other events which are likely to intrude during the research can help plan reading time. Certainly students would want to have their reading up-to-date before a tutor's visit to school so that any difficulties can be shared and resolved. Teachers would naturally plan their reading time away from parents' evenings or inspections unless these were integral to the research itself. This is a 'goes without saying' kind of point, but with many new things to consider it can be overlooked and lead to an overwork crisis.

And once the research is done, reflecting on the chosen literature and evaluating its relevance in the light of the findings is an important part of the penultimate chapter in a thesis. So don't stop reading or return your library books too soon.

A last word is to mention the tensions that can arise at the reading stage. It is tempting to keep reading and looking for more information, but this has to be weighed up against actually setting pen to paper and getting on with the investigation. On the other hand the temptation may be to start the action part of the investigation too soon, before the groundwork is fully prepared. That can cause real frustration if, as the research unfolds, the revelation of a 'better way' comes too late! It is a question of trying to find the best plan for the time available.

And of course reading is not just about the topic. Texts on research methodology need to be studied to ensure that the most appropriate strategies are used and that the chosen ones are well designed.

Writing a literature review

Now is the time to show how your investigation was guided and enlightened by the literature you read. In effect you are saying, 'Here is some of the recent advice on this topic and this is the way it guided my study.' The guidance leads to you making decisions about what is to be investigated (the research question) and how this is to be done (the action plan). These decisions have to be set out so that the rationale for the new study in its context is understood. Harlen and Schlapp (1998) describe this process. They write: 'The guiding principle for providing a valuable literature review can be summarised as making all procedures and decisions explicit, so that readers can be clear about the evidence base on which the review is founded.'

And so in the review of literature chapter of a research report or thesis, you aim to show how your research question and subsequent action plan have come from studying the literature. If your review follows on from an introduction which explains the topic and the context briefly and also takes time to justify converting 'the idea' into an action research study, you will be able to go straight into the review with little preamble. If, on the other hand, the review is standing alone as a piece of work, you will need an explanatory introduction to set the investigation in context.

In either case, it could be appropriate to say something about the selection of texts which informed your work. Were many available and if so, by what criteria did you make your selection? Or if there were few, did you discover why? Was this a 'new' aspect of education, or perhaps an obscure or particularly difficult area? Your reader would be interested to know – always keeping an eye on your word limit.

It is certainly important to show that you have identified, understood and considered the relevance of complementary and conflicting ideas or stances within the texts that you have read. How should this be done? Stark (1998) advises readers to 'identify competing perspectives within the theme, set them out one against the other and then identify the strengths and weaknesses in the views given'. To fulfil this you need to record the relevant information you have gained from cross-referencing texts and from answering at least some of the questions (see p.16). These were prepared to ensure that the criteria, 'reading critically and analytically' were fulfilled.

Perhaps you followed the advice given on (p.20) and began reading the key texts with a set of three or four questions prepared so that the answers would provide a structure to your review? If you did, you might like to begin by writing something like:

> This review is structured around answering three questions chosen to enlighten the intervention process. They are, (to give just one example),
> 1. What is Play?
> 2. Should teachers intervene in children's play?
> 3. What intervention strategies have been evaluated as being conducive to learning?
>
> Question 1: What is Play?

And so on, answering each question in turn. And as you do, consider the word length for this section of the thesis and subdivide it so that the review is balanced. This kind of structure enables the reader to anticipate what could be in each part of the review and this is very helpful. It also allows you to insert or delete parts of each answer without disturbing the flow of the whole text.

When you prepare to write, one of the difficulties is to know how many quotations to use. Certainly you want credit for all the reading you have done, but a good review is not a series of quotations linked together by a few words. If this 'diamond necklace approach' is used, and especially if there is difficult terminology, the reader cannot discern whether the meaning within the literature has been understood. To overcome this, it is better to paraphrase or explain the author's meaning in your own words, interspersing just a few quotations if they are particularly apt, especially revealing or if you consider that the author has put over the point succinctly and in language which could not be bettered.

The amount of explanation which needs to accompany a quote depends on the complexity of the language which has been used, but it is good to remember that the author's words have been quoted out of context and some explanation can help the reader understand how and why the words illustrate the point you are attempting to make.

N.B. Always check that you have enclosed the author's work in enough of your own to assure the reader that you understood what was being said, that you read the material in context, and that you did not simply grab a quotation that appeared to bear some relationship to the theme and then leave the reader to make the connection! If you are unsure whether to explain terminology or not, think of the reader as an educated lay person, i.e. someone who would readily understand 'group work' but perhaps not the meaning of 'epistemology'.

Example

If, for example, you were studying the development of the self-esteem in children, you might wish to report Gallahue and Ozmun's (1995) claim that, 'A child who feels worthless due to repeated failures often falls back on the strategy of deliberate failure which serves as a self-protective device.'

At first reading, this information may sound straightforward and self-explanatory, and the temptation may be to leave it in isolation. But if you do, how does the reader know if you understand? It would be much more useful to give a brief explanation of your understanding of why this deliberate failure strategy would be adopted by some children and how they could see it as 'self-protecting'. And so, although the terminology does not appear too difficult, there are still complexities in the claim which need to be teased out. Then you are sure to get credit for fully understanding the quotation.

In contrast, if a more taxing quote is used, e.g. 'Action research is concerned with exploring the multiple determinants of action, interactions and interpersonal relationships in unique contexts...' (Somekh 1995), the reader would want to know what you understood by 'the multiple determinants' and how you explained the way in which 'unique contexts influenced the interactions and relationships'. If this, i.e. knowing what to explain, seems difficult, look back at the first quote in this chapter and see how the essence of it has been explained. Did this help?

One of the important aspects of a review is that all details of the source materials are carefully recorded. Why would this be necessary? Well, you may have identified an interesting piece of work which the reader does not know and is fascinated to read. Or the reader may suspect you have quoted the author out of context and thus skewed the meaning. Only the original text can show if this is the case and accessing this may clarify the misunderstanding or explain the argument you are putting forward.

A critically important reason is that identifying other sources in this way means that you are acknowledging the original authors and showing that you are not claiming their work as your own. Failing to do this would lead to a charge of plagiarism. This is another reason for keeping exact details of original sources as you read, for as time passes and you read lots of articles, you may forget the derivation of some and unwittingly claim some other person's work as your own. You would be devastated by the plagiarism charge which could result, for 'not meaning to' is not accepted as an excuse!

One of the difficulties in compiling bibliographies is that different institutions and publishers have their preferred way of presenting details. They have their own 'house-style'. Usually there is minimal variation – all require full details, but the layout can vary. Some will not require page numbers to be included; some will require the key books to be listed under 'References', and others under 'Bibliography'; some prefer all books to be listed under the heading 'Bibliography'. Be sure to check and until you do, keep all the details safely. And once you have decided on a system or convention, be meticulous in using it as you proceed, for this will more than repay time in proofreading the work later on.

Below are examples of different kinds of excerpts from texts and one way of entering them into a bibliography.

A book
Maccoby, E.E. (1990) *Social Development: Psychological growth and the parent–child relationship*. New York: Harcourt Brace Jovanovich.
This is a straightforward recording of a book that was used. The author's name and place of publication is followed by the title in italics. Thereafter come the place where the book was published and finally the publisher's name.

A chapter within a book
Bradley, L. (1990) 'Rhyming connections in learning to read and spell', in Pumfrey, P.D. and Elliot, C.D. (eds) *Children's Difficulties in Reading, Spelling and Writing*. London: Falmer.
This example is slightly different because the work you actually used was in just one chapter of a book made up of a number of chapters all written by different people. The name of the author of your specific chapter goes first and then the chapter title in single quotes. Then the word 'in' indicates that the editor(s)' name(s) will be followed by the title of the book which is italicised. After that comes the place of publication and the publisher's name as before.

A journal article
Macintyre, C. (1998) 'Helping children with movement difficulties', *Education 3–13; The Professional Journal for Primary Education* **26**(1).
This shows how a journal article fares in the bibliography. It is almost the same as a book, but in this case, it is the title of the journal which is italicised. After the actual title come two other numbers. The first indicates the edition number, the second the issue. In this case there have been 25 previous editions and in the 26th, this is the first of three issues which will be produced in the year.

The examples here are not in alphabetical order because they are chosen to show variations, but alphabetical ordering is necessary in a final document – again to facilitate finding the original.

An article from a website
Stark, R. (1998) Practitioner research: The Purposes of Reviewing the Literature within an Inquiry. http://www.scre.ac.uk
As this article was downloaded from the web the website address replaces the publisher/place of publication.

There are variations in the way the detail is recorded and you have to check this with the awarding institution and/or any publisher. It is best to do this before you begin taking notes. The main thing is to be accurate and to highlight where the book, article or policy document may be found.

N.B. The Bibliography is very important. It shows care and discipline, and this is what research is all about!

And so in your review, you will be aiming to show how you have dealt with the themes outlined in the literature. Did you extend one particular facet of the work? Did you replicate part, but in a very different context? Or if there were contrasting claims put forward by different authors, which did you choose to develop? And why? Was it because you could visualise one way happening in your own context? Would that bias the results, do you think, or did you implement and evaluate one way in the light of the claims made by the other? Your reader will be pleased to see that not only have you considered different perspectives but you are thinking through the implications of choosing one mode of action instead of the other. Perhaps you discussed the authors' differences and offered a resolution or another way of tackling the issue in your own study? It is very important that you explain any background thinking, so that the reader can fully understand the decisions you made in relation to the place where they happened.

At the end of the review then, your reader should know:
- what the research topic is, and how it has been defined by different authors especially if they have interesting and possibly conflicting things to say;
- what aspect of the topic you have chosen to investigate, and why;
- what strategies others have tried and how they have worked;
- if and how contextual factors influenced these action plans;
and finally:
- how all of this information informed the new investigation.

This is encapsulated in the research question which now becomes the focus of the study.

CHAPTER 3

Formulating a research question

The research question is the central focus of your investigation. It must be clear, unambiguous and genuine i.e. not something obvious that can be answered 'yes' or 'no'; and if possible, concise! No wonder Dillon (1985) wrote, 'By the time of advanced graduate study, students have answered thousands upon thousands of questions, only to have a time of it thinking up a single question for their thesis.' Composing a good research question is tricky; it is not likely to spring to mind without considerable thought, reworking, rephrasing and piloting on willing friends to see if their interpretation matches your own.

Let's recap for a moment and ascertain your research stance at this moment in time, i.e. when you are ready to finalise your research question.

- You have reflected on your present classroom practice and decided what aspect you would choose to improve or extend.
- You have, from reading the literature and from your own experience in the classroom, considered in what ways this improvement would benefit the pupils in your class.
- You have discerned strategies which are likely to be helpful in bringing this improvement into being and you now wish to consider these in the context of your own research.

To form the research question these points need to be clearly defined, not remain as vague notions. How can this be done?

One helpful way is to write answers to four questions.

1. What exactly do I wish to find out?
2. In what ways should my teaching improve/be extended?
3. How will the pupils' learning be enhanced?
4. What strategies will I try to bring this about?

The answers to these questions can help formulate a comprehensive research question which asks, 'If I do this (i.e. make this change to extend my teaching), to what extent will this enable the children to do that (i.e. achieve the intended improvement)?'

This phraseology, setting out the question in three parts, provides a structure which is especially helpful when it comes to planning and later evaluating the research action, because then you can reflect on and evaluate each part in turn, i.e. your own input, the effectiveness of the strategies which were recommended by the literature or designed by you, and the pupils' responses to the change. The phrase 'to what extent' is important too, because it leaves room for different levels of attainment by different children. It also suggests that this is a genuine enquiry where the strategies will be carefully evaluated in context and that 'honest' findings will be reported.

Of course, research questions can be written more briefly, asking, e.g. 'In what ways does (the action) affect the participants or cause the pupils to —', but in my experience the more elaborate version reassures the less experienced researcher that all important areas have been covered and that the chance of ambiguity has been reduced.

The best way of avoiding ambiguity is to make explicit exactly what is to be investigated. This can also be called operationalising the research question. Let's consider a 'vague' question which needs further thought and then look at the improved version. A vague stage 1 question might be: 'If I involve children in a daily activity programme, will this improve their performance?'

Given this question I would first ask, how many children were to participate and was there any specific reason for choosing them? Secondly, did they need special input e.g. to overcome some disability, and if so, were all the children's needs the same? I would be helped by knowing the programme was to happen 'daily' but for how long and for how many weeks? Thirdly, what kind of activity was planned, and lastly, what kind of improvement was anticipated? Can you see how the question left the reader with a number of imponderables? The aim is to make all of these clear.

The stage 2 question which emerged from operationalising the question was:

If I involve four children with poor fine motor control in a planned series of activities (e.g. 20 minutes daily for 6 weeks) specially designed to improve fine motor skills, will this help their letter formation as they write?

Can you see the extra thinking that went into this exemplification and do you see how it provides a clear statement of intention? You may be surprised at the number of sessions, but changes can take time. Also if the researcher is reporting improvement, then it has to be observed over time, not on just one occasion. It could also be important for some research to have observations in different environments. Better to plan for extra time than discover there isn't enough to make valid claims about the results.

In most research with children, it is important to consider the composition of the study group. Is the whole class to be involved or just one group and is the composition of that group important e.g. being made up of high attainers or children who need extra help? Or is the selected group representative of the class? Perhaps the whole class is to be involved so that no-one feels left out, but only certain children are to be closely monitored? Knowing this kind of detail lets the reader envisage the scale of the research, points to the kind of data gathering which could be feasible and manageable and allows some anticipation of possible outcomes.

The issue of feasibility and manageability links to the time-scale of the project and although this may not appear in the question, the parameters of what is envisaged certainly affect the numbers which can be accommodated, the number of data gathering sessions, the opportunities for others to make observations to confirm the findings – in other words, all features of the action plan.

Formulating an interesting and potentially useful research question is a critical part of the research process because the research action is planned to provide evidence or data to answer that question. No other information, no matter how diverting, contributes to the research. The findings must answer the research question. If it is amended in context in response to what has been discovered, then that is a positive step, but the researcher(s) must make a conscious decision about the change and record the reasons why. They mustn't just drift into something different because the first plan has run into difficulties. The penalty for doing that is finding that there is no evidence to answer the research question – and sadly, no means of discovering why!

Examples of research questions

Example 1. Topic: Gender bias in discussion. Researcher: Ray

Ray's research question was: 'If I develop discussion topics in single sex trios and gradually, over five short sessions, change this to mixed groups, to what extent will this enable three reluctant-to-participate girls to contribute in whole-class discussions?'

Ray was concerned that in his class of twelve-year-olds, three bright but shy girls were reluctant to volunteer any contributions in class discussions and as a result, their oral assessments were not a reflection of their true ability.

Reflection caused Ray to admit that the discussion topics could have exacerbated this. He had chosen topics where he had some depth of knowledge so that he could input relevant information and cope with the pupils' different views. However, he recognised that these topics were biased towards the boys' interests. And so, for the improvement/extension of his own performance, he sought to alter this by organising the class in small single-sex groups and allowing each group to select a topic from a given list.

Although the whole class participated in this organisation, and he ostensibly recorded each group's input, he concentrated on observing and carefully monitoring the three girls, each in a different group. None of the other children was aware of this.

He discovered that although each of the girls was willing to speak at some length in their small group discussions, the introduction of two boys put paid to that. And this was despite the 'successful' topic being retained, for Ray had asked the girls to share their conclusions with the boys, thinking that this would give them confidence. He had discovered that for this group, the topic choice was not the enabling factor he had anticipated. So what now?

He went back to the literature and this time focused on how friendships are formed. He discovered, through reading Maccoby (1990), that the modes of interaction in some boys' and girls' groups are very different – the boys having a more aggressive style. Enlightened by this he held small group interviews with all of the groups and found that the shy girls were afraid of contributing because, 'they'll just laugh even though they don't know as much as us' and 'they'll tease us in the playground'. 'They'll shout out, "Ho, Ho, listen to the know-it-alls".' The girls had decided that it was much better to stay silent!

And so Ray had to report that for this particular group of girls, neither of his theories had proved correct. Neither the choice of topic nor the new organisation was conducive to the girls speaking out.

And when he came to evaluate, he reflected on how he had put the idea over to the class and the strategy he tried (i.e. what he did). He then evaluated his method of data collection as well as the findings, (i.e. how the action plan had affected the girls who were to have made the improvement). Although his plan hadn't 'worked' in the sense of achieving his first anticipated outcome he had found out why. This was good research, and he was determined to find alternative ways to assess the oral competence of the three girls.

Example 2. Topic: Expressiveness in dance/drama and story writing. Researcher: Catriona

As another example, let's follow Catriona through the process of developing a research question. At her first discussion she explained that she wished to use a multimedia approach to develop creativity in her pupils, so that she could discover whether, without prompting, the pupils would transfer learning from one expressive arts activity to another. If they did, then there was the possibility of all-round improvement in their creative work. Her class of nine-year-olds, 15 girls and 14 boys, had just had a year when literacy and numeracy were stressed, and in Catriona's view they were 'technically competent but without imagination'. She wished to redress the balance. She met her tutor to discuss her plan and clarify her thinking, and the following dialogue took place (T=Tutor, C=Catriona):

T: What exactly do you want to find out?

C: If I develop lessons in the expressive arts – in language, dance/drama and art – will the children transfer their learning from one medium to another – automatically, without prompting that is…?

T: How would that help your teaching?

C: Well, I would be involved in thematic planning within the expressive arts and that would be a new experience for me. I know I said that the children would make the transfer of learning without prompting, but the separate inputs would need to be planned so that there was a logical possibility of letting that happen – some link which would allow the children to make a connection. I haven't tried that before.

T: How will the children benefit?

C: By having a concentrated input in the expressive arts, their innate creativity should be boosted and hopefully this should enable them to produce more creative work across the curriculum.

Catriona was reassured that she had made an interesting and worthwhile choice of topic and advised that the next stage involved focusing her reading and also considering the parameters of what she was attempting to do. Would she perhaps start by studying the transfer between just two of the expressive arts, given that she had to design and implement data gathering strategies as the children worked? She went off to consider.

At this stage, she had browsed through some journals in the Arts and the relevant curriculum guidelines but her literature search needed to be focused, so she prepared questions to help her look for specific advice from the literature. These were:

- What is creativity?
- Can children be creative?
- What kind of 'classroom' organisation will help children to be creative?

Catriona found some of the literature, 'especially journals about the aesthetic domain', very difficult. However, she claimed to have enough straightforward advice to make a start. What was the essence of that advice?

The answer to the first question found that although creativity, in the past, had been regarded as something magical and mysterious, it was now considered to be 'an aspect of development which was waiting to be developed just like any other' (Abbs 1985). This gave Catriona confidence that every child could benefit from her input.

Answering the second question made her reconsider her terminology and use 'imaginative' rather than 'creative'. This was because she doubted whether children could meet the criteria for being creative. From other research she had devised criteria for the four stages of the creative process and she called these, 'finding a problem', 'pondering', and this she described as a lengthy period of contemplation, 'illumination', which was the 'eureka' feeling when the right answer appeared and 'verification', which meant that the created piece had to be able to stand scrutiny by someone learned in the field. As a result Catriona now anticipated work which was imaginative rather than creative, new to them, rather than original, and self-expressive, i.e. expressing their feelings and emotions, rather than being art-expressive, i.e. expressing the art form.

Remembering these criteria however, had helped her answer her final question because she realised how long the children would need to develop and refine their ideas. She also realised that the children were unlikely to be able to be imaginative to order, that is, that they could not all sit and produce pieces of imaginative writing derived from work in dance/drama at one specific time. She decided to have an integrated day kind of organisation. Then the children could decide to write when they had time to think and when their imaginations were most fertile.

All of this had let her see that her original plans, i.e. to involve all the expressive arts, were far too ambitious and so she limited her study to studying the transfer of learning between dance/drama in the gym and imaginative writing in the classroom. The idea that the transfer should come from the children remained.

Research question, stage 1

'If I teach imaginative work in dance/drama to what extent will this enable the children to write imaginative stories on a similar theme?'

The investigation was taking shape but still needed more focus. Questions to achieve this were:

- What would be the focus of the imaginative work in drama?
- What were the imaginative stories to be about?
- What kind of link were the children likely to be able to make?

Catriona's answers

1. As this will happen in the autumn term, the dance/drama theme will be about bonfire night. The children can act out a scene of fireworks around a bonfire. The rockets can swoosh, the catherine wheels twirl and spin, the bangers can pop and explode, the flames in the fire can leap and twist and the smoke can eddy and swirl. It will be a dark misty night and the children can develop a story, perhaps about a grumpy park keeper who thinks the bonfire party should be cancelled, and a young boy who defies him and lights the bonfire. Sparks then set the bonfire alight...

2. The theme for the imaginative writing will be 'Lost on a November night'. The children are to imagine that they are lost in the mist and describe how this happened; how they felt; what they saw and how they got home.

3. The link is in the similar storyline of the two learning experiences and the emphasis on expressive language which could be used in both scenarios.

The final research question

'If I build a series of four dance/drama lessons on the theme 'Bonfire Night', and stress action words, to what extent will this stimulate the children to transfer their learning and write imaginatively on a similar theme, "Lost on a November night"?'

And once the question was finalised, the lessons and data gathering strategies (video for the dance/drama and uncorrected pieces of story writing for the language), were planned and implemented.

The findings showed that while some of the children wrote fluently and expressively, using many of the descriptive words which had been stressed in the dance/drama, other children had obviously compartmentalised their learning and made no connection between the two activities. Interestingly, when Catriona drew their attention to the possibility of using the link, most could do it – but they needed the teacher to show how the transfer of learning could work. One or two children who struggled with writing anyway seemed unable to make any kind of transfer at all.

More examples of research questions

Topic: 'Reading' through picture books. Class: Infant 1

'If I model describing pictures so that each character and aspects of the background are enveloped in imaginative words, to what extent will this help my children to tell fuller imaginative stories of their own?'

Topic: Understanding mathematical language. Class: Infant 2

'If four children who are experiencing difficulty with maths language (e.g. 'more than'; 'subtraction') are involved in group activities using concrete materials, in what ways will their conceptual understanding be enhanced?'

Topic: Gender bias in the development of fine motor skills. Class: Infant 3

'If I set up daily fine motor skill practices in the classroom, to what extent will this transfer to help the writing ability of two girls and two boys who are finding pencil control difficult?'

Topic: Colour and emotion. Class: Primary 4

'If I introduce a colour vocabulary, linking a colour to a particular emotion, will this enable children to talk about the feelings depicted in their art work?'

Topic: Discussion and collaborative group work. Class: Primary 7

'If the children learn to discuss, and through that the social skills of turn taking and listening to others, will this enable them to collaborate in craft activities, i.e. will there be transfer of social learning?'

Topic: Extending able children through problem solving in mathematics. Class: Primary 7

'If able children are made aware of the effective and less effective problem solving strategies they use, will their ability to differentiate enable them to select appropriately when they encounter more challenging mathematical problems?'

Topic: Peer assessment and imaginative writing.
Class: Primary 7

'If I provide a list of criteria covering issues such as character descriptions, will this enable the children to make appropriate assessments of each other's work?'

The research question(s) are very important for they indicate what evidence is to be gathered, how this is to be done, and as a result, what claims can be justifiably made at the end of it all. In the final writing up, the question stays as the central focus and all the explanations, justifications and claims must be logically connected! (See p.100)

As the research question is formulated, the researchers must ask themselves, 'How am I going to answer this question?' i.e. what teaching input is necessary to cover the 'If I do' part of the question, and what kind of evidence will I need to collect to show 'to what extent' the improvement has occurred? One way is to find the hypotheses or testable ideas which are implicit in each part of the research question and identify the categories of evidence which are to be monitored. This is quite complex, but it pays dividends at the data analysis stage when the evidence is tightly tied to the question. In this way the data or evidence produces valid explanations of why the change did or did not work.

Research questions and (implicit) hypotheses which identify categories for data collection

The following examples show how to find hypotheses within a research question and how they may be used to define categories for the collection of data.

Example 1. Teacher: Ian. Topic: Becoming critical readers.
Class: Primary 5

The research question was: 'If I involve the children in a series of reading activities where they must differentiate between facts and opinions, to what extent will this enable them to read newspapers "critically" i.e. understanding how opinions can blur the truth?' The implicit hypotheses are marked *, followed by identification of the categories for data collection.

1. *that I will be able to explain the differences clearly and consistently through different activities.

Category: Clear explanations. The data will be collected by tape recordings and the class teacher's evaluations of the explanations that were made.

2. *that P5 children will be able to differentiate between fact and opinion in different genres.

Category: Ability to differentiate. The data will be collected by gathering examples of the children's oral and written work (see examples).

3. *that the children will collect adverts which provide good discussion material for the class.

Category: Participation. The data will be based on the children's collecting adverts and being able to justify their choice (see example).

4. *that as a result of this input, the children will be able to read a local newspaper item critically, discerning the difference between facts and opinions.

Category: Transfer of learning. The children's ability to differentiate between fact and opinion will be tape-recorded during individual teacher/pupil interactions.

Examples

The first example (Figure 3.1) was taken as a lighthearted class discussion where the children could draw from their own experiences, compare ideas in the text to their own and then discuss whether, in the light of the views put forward by the class, these could be classified as facts or opinions.

The second example (Figure 3.2) was a number of statements prepared by Ian and the children wrote their answers individually. These were collected as evidence, and then, after Ian had collated the 'anonymous' results, the tallies were discussed as a class activity. This reinforced the differences between fact and fiction.

The third example was an advertisement. As this was done on January 25th i.e. Burns night, and as the children were having Irn Bru at their Burns supper, the well known television advert brought in by Jennifer was discussed. It was:

Irn Bru – Scotland's National Drink – Made from Girders!

The children discussed issues such as, 'could the retailers legitimately claim Irn Bru as Scotland's national drink'? What effect would this have on sales? What was implied by "being made from girders"? Was there an

A Grandmother is a lady who has no children of her own, so she likes other people's little girls and boys. A grandfather is a man grandmother. He goes for walks with the boys and they talk about fishing and tractors. Grandmothers don't have to do anything but be there. They are old, so they shouldn't play hard or run. They should never say 'Hurry up'. Usually they are fat, but not too fat to tie children's shoes. They wear glasses and funny underwear, and they can take their teeth and gums off. They don't have to be smart, only answer questions like why cats hate dogs and why God isn't married. They don't talk baby-talk like visitors. When they read to us, they don't skip bits, or mind if it is the same story over again. Everybody should have one, especially if you don't have television, because grandmothers are the only grown-ups who have time.

By an eight-year-old

Figure 3.1

FACT OR OPINION

Read each of the sentences below and decide whether they are facts or opinions. Underline what you think is a fact in BLUE and then underline what you think is an opinion in RED.

1. The car was blue.
2. The man had lost his coat.
3. Chester City is the best football club in the world.
4. It's not a very good telvision programme.
5. Westlife's single was the most popular over Christmas.
6. I believe that he can win.
7. Pete Sampras is the best tennis player there has ever been.
8. Pete Sampras, the tennis player, is the World number one.
9. We think that Mark stole the car.
10. I did not have a coat.
11. The church is the tallest building in town.
12. You might get wet if you forget your coat.

Figure 3.2   Differentiating between fact and opinion

implied link between the rusty colour of the liquid and the strength of the girders? What were the facts and what were the opinions and could the children grasp the marketing techniques which were in play?'

Ian reported his research to the other teachers in the school. He evaluated what he had done by showing his data gathering instruments on overhead projector. This was an attempt to share his ideas before writing his thesis.

Example 2. Teacher: Laura. Topic: Improving fine motor control to help writing. Class: Primary 5

The research question was: 'If I involve four children with poor fine motor control in a planned series of activities (20 minutes daily for 6 weeks) specially designed to improve fine motor skills, will this help their writing in the classroom?' The implicit hypotheses are marked *, folllowed by identification of the categories for data collection.

1. *that daily activity sessions of 20 minutes will strengthen Ben's arms, Jan's finger grip and Ian's shoulder control.

Category: Strength. The data will be gathered by testing strength before the activity sessions begin, during the programme and at the end. The children will be asked information about any other concurrent activities which might contribute to strengthening.

2. *that children will sustain their interest and participate well.

Category: Participation. The data will be gathered by observing the children each day, noting their attendance and keeping tabs on their level of participation. Other teachers will regularly observe the quality of the programme.

3. *that the improvement in fine motor skills in the gym will transfer to the classroom particularly to improve the writing ability of the children.

Category: Writing skill. The data will be gathered by collecting examples of the children's writing over the weeks of the programme.

This ongoing analysis, i.e. 'What exactly do I want to find out', has been followed by the question, 'How will I know if this has been achieved?' The categories are the data descriptors, or the points to be monitored, and they form the nucleus of the action plan.

Formulating a hypothesis

A hypothesis is: 'a tentative proposition which is subject to verification through subsequent investigation' (Verma and Beard 1981).

An alternative model to the research question is one based on the formulation of an hypothesis, i.e. a testable idea. Usually a relationship between two variables is postulated (e.g. If I do X then Y results) and then tested by gathering evidence. The hypothesis-testing procedure is often selected if the researcher has a realistic notion of what the outcome of the investigation could be or if one procedure only is to be investigated.

In this mode the researcher may wish to test someone else's research findings in their own context. The new investigation may then add to or detract from the credibility of the original research or extend the knowledge base. It is a model which, in stipulating the outcome in advance, denies any alteration or amendment during the process of the research. The hypothesis is either confirmed or denied and the evidence to support or negate the claim is clearly documented. As with the research question model, the hypothesis emerges from reading the literature, reflecting on experience and from discussion with people knowledgeable in the field.

Examples

1. 'That the use of higher-order questions will stimulate the pupils to give resourceful responses.' In this investigation, the researcher would carefully monitor the pupils' responses to prepared higher order questions. This would test the hypothesis.

Action: Preparation of higher-order questions. Organisation and recording of teacher/pupil interaction. Evaluation.

If longer and more thoughtful responses occurred, then the hypothesis was confirmed (i.e., for these pupils in that particular situation). If no improvement took place, then the hypothesis was denied. Once the result was known and the reasons investigated, the researcher would not go on to try out other ways of stimulating responses...only the research question would have this kind of flexibility.

2. a) 'That pupils in P4 will be able to articulate the criteria they use to assess their creative writing.'

   b) 'That there will be a match between the pupils' and the teacher's choice.'

3. 'That "social worries" will outweigh "academic worries" in pupils anticipating transition to secondary school.'

If, as in Example 3, the variables could be open to misinterpretation, they should be carefully explained. This procedure is called 'operationalising the hypothesis'. For example, academic worries could be specified as:

1. new subjects;
2. not coping;
3. poor marks.

Social worries could be specified as:

1. bullying;
2. failure to make friends;
3. getting lost.

In some ways the two strategies are similar, i.e., they both require the researcher to narrow down their field until particular variables or questions have been identified. They differ however in the timing of the final version – the research question model having the capacity to react to the pupils' unexpected responses or to the teachers' shifting the focus or locus of their investigation. This involves amending the question to take account of developments as they occur.

Just before looking at different ways of gathering data, there are some other aspects which need to be considered so that the action research plan can go ahead confidently and ethically.

Ethical considerations

Before moving on to 'planning the action in the school context', it behoves us to take some time to consider the ways and means of ensuring that the whole process will be ethically sound and cause no distress to any of the participants, either in school or in the wider community.

There are several factors which allow action research in the classroom to get off to a good start. Firstly, it is designed to make things better and surely no-one could object to that? And secondly, teachers know their pupils well and can anticipate any subtle, negative effects of change e.g. even the upset which could result from changing a group arrangement. Furthermore, these experienced teachers will oversee their students' research plans and in giving their approval or asking for a change, accept or reject the research idea for their children in their classroom. But the plan on paper may develop in unforeseen ways. It is difficult for anyone investigating something new to anticipate exactly what will happen, and so constant care is the name of the game.

N.B. Those in authority have to know what is happening in their own school, for only then can they foresee the implications of any proposed change.

Observe protocol

The first 'rule' is to give everyone who is to be involved as clear a picture as possible of the research topic, the action plan, the people who will be involved and the means by which data will be collected. This is one reason why 'as-detailed-as-possible planning' before beginning any action is essential. And once the plans are written, they have to be adhered to. Given the propensity for action research to alter focus or amend original plans once the action unfolds, this is difficult, but keeping those in authority informed is a courtesy expected from any guest in the school and prevents any backlash later.

Although this extra writing may seem unnecessary, even tedious, it can help the researcher to clarify and justify the purpose of the research and therefore contribute to the final report. Keeping a copy of any communication is another good idea, for busy teachers who may have to cover for another class and not be present during all the research actions, and head teachers, faced with parents demanding to know what is going on, may well forget they have been informed!

Altering the original plans needs to be carefully considered too. Mid-research, the researcher may have a 'breakthrough idea' which involves asking the parents their opinions/feelings/ideas. At the very least, the head teacher's permission has to be gained before the parents are approached and this takes time. Then there is all the organisation involved in getting letters home and usually more frustration in getting the replies back. Furthermore, if a questionnaire is planned, the researcher has to realise that it is difficult and time-consuming to compose one which will give meaningful results. Will student researchers have the authority to act on them anyway? What, for example, could you do, if the parents you contacted disapproved of the literacy hour or taking the children out of school to go swimming or resented homework projects? Even passing this kind of information up the ladder can be a thankless task if the suggestions cross school policy or if those in authority would rather not know.

There are two important points here. Researchers must work within the 'general procedures of the organisation' (Hopkins 1994). The school is likely to have a planned mechanism for introducing and evaluating any important change and will know, ahead of time, why, how and when this is to be done. Any research must must respect this and not pre-empt change or cut across any other plans.

The second point concerns what researchers can expect others to do. This may cause a great deal of resentment, particularly at the data collection stage. Other teachers may have responded positively to an earlier informal request to make observations of children working – to reduce bias in the collection of data (see p.43) – or they may have agreed to cover groups to let the researcher concentrate on just one. However, other pressures may have made this difficult at the 'right' time and, for a whole host of reasons, 'promises' made earlier may not be kept. This can affect the research and the researcher badly. So giving gentle reminders in plenty of time is a good strategy.

Perhaps other teachers or classroom assistants or nursery nurses agreed to be interviewed and find, quite against their expectations of spending ten minutes, that they have to sit for an hour. They can be understandably annoyed. Or perhaps a lengthy questionnaire has, in the recipients' eyes, irritating, poorly constructed questions which ask for obvious answers, or perhaps they probe too far? It is not easy to get the balance right and anticipate all the nuances of the research action.

Decentre

Possibly the best way to avoid these difficulties is for the researchers to decentre, i.e. to put themselves in the place of the children, the parents, or the other teachers and to try to appreciate the demands and subtleties of the research and the added stress these could cause. Consider the following two examples.

1. Rob had chosen 'Introducing self-assessment in mathematics' as his research topic. He wanted to find if ten-year-old children were able to identify and evaluate the problem-solving strategies they used. He hoped that developing this kind of metacognition might reinforce his teaching points and so lead to the pupils improving their skill. He decided to pilot this idea on a small group of very able children first, before involving different ability groups. He hadn't considered it necessary to explain this organisation to the children, not realising that they would report their own version of events home. And so he was surprised and dismayed to find parents clamouring to find why their children had been excluded from the 'top group', which, according to the children, was having extra coaching!

2. Sally decided to video her four-year-old nursery children playing. She wanted to collect data on how they played to see if they were practising learned skills or developing new competences, i.e. she wished to differentiate between ludic and epistemic behaviour (Hutt 1979) as a way of justifying intervention in the children's play. She had decided that the video replay facility would be a useful and unobtrusive means of studying the children as it had been used recently without seeming to cause any ill effects. The film would show whether they were repeating actions, which might justify her

intervening, or whether they were discovering new things on their own, and in that case she might decide to stay back.

Repeated viewings of the video, however, showed up additional and unexpected things. Two of the children were having difficulty coordinating their actions They were very clumsy as they moved around, often stumbling for no apparent reason. Fitting parts of the jigsaw together was difficult too and was quickly abandoned; controlling a pencil and paint brush was ineffective as the children clutched with their whole hands rather than using the pincer grip. Seeing this, the nursery staff decided that the boys would benefit from extra specialist help and contacted their parents, expecting that they would be glad to have this information before the boys started primary school. Not so! The parents were very upset and asked why they had not been informed that their children were being filmed for diagnostic purposes. One set thought that 'it is ridiculous to label children at four years old', and the other, obviously misunderstanding the school's concern, dismissed the findings out of hand, 'I know my son, he's a bright lad. I'm his Mother after all.' The parents were also anxious to know who else had seen the film. The staff understood that any suggestion that the boys had a difficulty would be a disappointment for the parents, but hadn't anticipated such a negative, aggressive response.

Ponder for a moment on this scenario. Were the parents' reactions acceptable? Was it ethical to video the children without consulting them – or was this an unreasonable idea? Was it ethical for the research to discover a difficulty and then not let the parents know or do nothing to alleviate it? Or should the staff have tried to give extra help unobtrusively? But what if they did not feel qualified to do this? Or what if they raised the possibility of specialist help with the parents and then, and this is likely, it could not be obtained? Were the teachers justified in making and recording these assessments if nothing could be done? Or was it letting the other staff know which annoyed the parents?

I have raised a hornets' nest of questions. They are not meant to dismay – only to show that good intentions are not always perceived as such! And so it is best to proceed with caution, checking procedures at each step of the way.

Confidentiality

'Letting others know' raises the question of confidentiality. Researchers usually reassure all the participants that the research will be confidential and by that they mean that the process and results will, in the first instance, be made known only to those intimately involved in the research. This is to allow the participants to act or reply 'as honestly as possible' so that the researchers can gain a true picture of events.

Anonymity

The second assurance is that in any reporting, the names and location will be changed so that no-one can identify where or with whom the research occurred. Having given these assurances, the researchers must do everything in their power to keep them. This sounds quite straightforward, but how easy is it to be private in a school where everyone is anxious to know how you are getting on or how things are progressing? How difficult is it not to share findings when you have discovered something fascinating or when a child has responded in an unexpectedly positive way? And if the head teacher asks about specific children, can you really say you don't know?

Certainly it is possible to keep field notes private and to make observations unobtrusively, but if the children suss out what is happening, should they be asked not to tell? Should they know about the research from the outset or would this cause them to alter their behaviour and bias the results? Again these issues need to be considered. Many may not cause problems at all, but it is better to visualise and take steps to avert difficulties than to be faced with the unexpected as the research proceeds. *N.B. Consider the promises you make in the light of those you will be able to keep!*

Studying children

The classroom is a favourable place for action research. The subjects are there, all tidily organised in age groups and possibly subdivided in other ways helpful to research enquiries. Unless the children are ill, they attend and this is important for continuity. Moreover they are usually lively, good humoured subjects, interested in anything new. They are unlikely or even unable to say 'no'. But these facts can leave them open to exploitation and researchers must be sure that children's rights are not infringed.

Action research in the classroom sets out to make things better, but research time will have impinged on teaching time will it not? What if the improvement will only help specific groups, perhaps the most or least able? What then? Can it still be justified? what if the research starts out with admirable intentions but the planned strategy doesn't work? Is finding out why something doesn't succeed just as helpful and important? Another difficult question concerns 'secrecy'. Should you tell the children the details of the research? Or should you keep silent to avoid the children altering their behaviour and thus distorting the results?

Bias

Promises of confidentiality and anonymity are made to allow those being observed, interviewed or given questionnaires to answer 'honestly' without fear of any reprisal. The hope is that these kinds of answers can prevent the replies adding bias or in some way distorting the research findings. This could occur if the respondents tried to anticipate the kinds of answer the researcher wanted to hear and replied accordingly. The research aim is to gather a 'normal', usual picture of events, where bias is reduced.

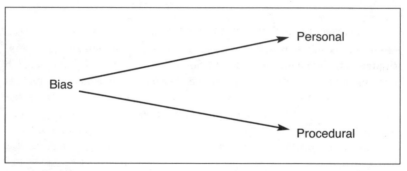

Figure 3.3 Sources of bias

It is not possible to eliminate bias completely because it is inherent in all research personnel and procedures (see Figure 3.3): in the choice of questions you ask, (why these and not others?), in the observations you make, (why then, not now? why that, not this?). Even the interpretation of the data could be biased because of your own value stance, your experience, your skill in making observations and your assumptions about the children in your class! Researchers have to be aware of all these variables and do their best to control them, for all research procedures have inbuilt bias if they distort the usual run of events. This is why data is best gathered in different ways by different people, perhaps even by the children themselves. In that way, different 'eyes', seeing things from different perspectives, have been used to check out the responses and endorse the findings or cause them to be reconsidered. This is called triangulation (see Figure 3.4).

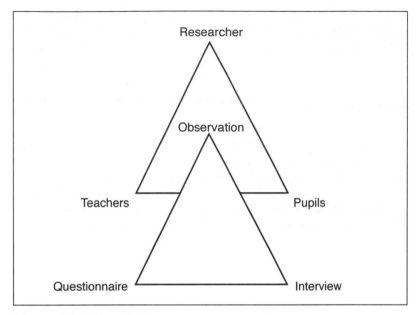

Figure 3.4 Triangulation

All of this detail must be reported in the writing up. Any reader who is to fully appreciate all the planning that was done to keep the research ethical, needs a full description of events, including all the measures which were taken to reduce bias. More detail on personal and procedural bias accompanies the different data gathering procedures.

Reliability

Reducing bias goes some way towards making the research reliable. This means that if another researcher was to duplicate the same investigation, the results would be the same. Or if the same questions were asked at another moment in time, then the answers would stay true.

As soon as questions are formulated, it is a good idea to pilot them on friends and ask them, if they will, to write brief answers. This serves two purposes. First it shows whether the questions mean the same to others as they do to you, and second, it shows the kind of answers (data) which the questions will bring in. Many a researcher who has tried this has been amazed at the 'misinterpretations' others make, and on scrutinising the answers has found that the data didn't enlighten the research at all! Better to pilot questions early than to be left asking, 'Why did they tell me that?' when it is too late to do anything about it.

In the classroom there are lots of measures which can be taken to try to foster reliability, e.g. not gathering data as the children are rushing off to go swimming, in case they write 'anything' just to escape, or avoiding asking for personal views on emotive issues just after a television programme has raised the tenor in a certain way, or not asking about teeth cleaning habits just as the dental van draws into the playground. Anticipating aspects of the action plan which could affect reliability and taking steps to reduce them is the best way forward.

There are many dilemmas to be resolved before moving into the action plan. Researchers plan a change then consider all the influences which could affect it, so that their eventual claims can be justified. It can be difficult to be sure what caused a change. Was the children's interest, attention and improvement caused by the novelty of being involved in research rather than the inherent worth of the innovation itself? There are no easy answers, but following the principles and procedures of action research can help to get it right.

Validity

The question of validity is difficult and complex. However, a small-scale piece of classroom research is not usually attempting to produce scales or tests which must stand statistical analysis, and so does not have that worry. Observing all the principles and constantly asking the following questions does give a measure of validity. These are:

- Are the questions clearly formulated so that the answers will provide data to illuminate the research question(s)?
- Are the procedures clear so that all stages of the investigation can be evaluated in context?
- Have steps to reduce bias and help reliability been taken?
- Can the claims that are made be 'legitimately' derived from the question(s), the action plan, and the evidence which was gathered?

In other words, are the claims valid?

Negotiating access

Teachers carrying out research within the confines of their own environment have the advantage of being familiar with the culture, the people, the policies, the routines, in fact the whole ethos of the school. Student teachers have benefits too, because the school has accepted them under an arrangement or contract which should allow them time for research and some support in carrying it out.

But of course, researchers may wish to investigate issues across schools, perhaps to have more children to enlarge the database or to compare the results from children of different social backgrounds, e.g. to look at the language development of children from advantaged and disadvantaged backgrounds at school entry. Or perhaps researchers would like to find out more about the community in which their pupils live with a view to discover e.g. if and when the children use the leisure resources which are available, if libraries are willing to share resources and facilities, if some artistic children might contribute to the development of the local Arts Festival or whether older children could be given some work experience? The wider community houses many possibilities.

Whatever the reason or the topic, if the research is to cross the school boundaries, access must be checked early, in fact as soon as a project plan has enough detail to let the invited 'partner' visualise what will be involved. For no matter how good the idea, no-one can assume that it can go ahead. The other school or library or arts group may just have started a project on their own; they may know a staff member is about to leave and doubt if a replacement will appear; the research idea may not be so suitable in their different context. There are lots of genuine reasons 'why not'. It does not mean that the research idea was a poor one.

Giving plenty of time to consider means that the implications of agreement can be carefully examined and that no-one is forced into accepting an innovation they would rather have refused. Considered acceptance will repay the early preparation in terms of the smooth running of the investigation once it is underway. On the other hand, the other participants(s) may suggest an amendment – even an improvement – or they may wish to interact as co-researchers rather than implementing someone else's plan. The home researcher has to be aware of these possible replies and in turn visualise the implications for the original idea.

This leads to the question of how much detail needs to be provided. It is frustrating in the extreme to have conceptualised, even costed a splendid plan and then the 'other' refuses to let it happen or, in the case of competing institutions bidding for a research grant, the time and money is awarded elsewhere. But of course no-one will accept a tentative, hastily drawn up set of 'maybes' either. Certainly, if others are to be persuaded to join in, they need a clear description of the topic, to know how many people are to be involved, how long the research will last, what kinds of questions will be asked and how the data is to be collected. A copy of any questionnaire or interview schedule is likely to be requested, for this is a good way of understanding the essence of the research and the parameters of the action. A critically important question will concern the findings. What is to happen to the data and, especially in this age of appraisal, who will get to know?

Once more, this raises the important issues of confidentiality and anonymity. Again assurances about outsiders not being able to identify the place or the people have to be given and the research practice has to ensure that these promises are kept. The 'home' researcher may wish to 'subtly' inform the other about protocol because if *they* break confidentiality, and in a collaborative venture there are more people to let this happen, then the integrity of the research may be jeopardised.

It is important to remember that all the people who contribute to your research are doing you a favour. At the very least they deserve a clear explanation of why they are being asked to participate and given that they are spending time to help, they need to know the purpose of the research and possibly how it may affect their children. It can also be politic to offer some reciprocation. And if you are a student carrying out research for the award of a degree, say so, because the recipients of your requests are likely to be sympathetic.

Let's see how one student and then a class teacher approached 'outsiders' to ask them to contribute to their research.

Example 1

Robbie's research was about parental involvement. The school were happy for him to approach their parents after the letters home had been scrutinised by the head teacher. She had initially been concerned that Robbie would suggest something which would interest the parents but which could not be accommodated by the school. However, after persuading Robbie that he should refrain from contacting all the parents and limit his enquiry to one age group, she was less concerned that the school might be swamped by volunteer helpers.

The letter home

Dear Mr and Mrs Smith
Thank you very much for taking the time and trouble to complete this questionnaire. I am a final year teacher-education student and part of my final qualification depends on my completing a piece of research. I have chosen the topic of parental involvement in school and I am trying to find if parents of primary 7 children wish to be involved in school life, and if they do, what aspect(s) they would like

---

> to support. The information will be used to help me to make plans so that people can do what they wish. All replies are confidential and no-one will be able to identify individual replies.
>
> Yours sincerely

The introductory statement is brief, just covering main purpose of the research. Explaining the research in context and assuring potential respondents that their replies will be treated confidentially should put them at their ease and encourage them to participate. The reciprocation was that prior organisation would make their time in school interesting, because their wishes, in terms of what they wanted to do, would be granted.

Example 2
This example covers a sensitive subject and so the parents need a longer description of what is to happen. The teacher is asking the parents' permission for their children to be involved in a new programme, informing them as to the content and offering them the opportunity to see the questionnaire which the pupils will be asked to complete.

The letter home

Dear Mrs Jones,
In school we are planning a new Health Education programme for Jamie's year group. Before this happens, and to ensure that the material is entirely appropriate, we anticipate carrying out a piece of research based on the following questions.
  (1) What do the children already know about the harmful effects of smoking and has this influenced their intention to try?
  (2) What do the children understand about the use of medicinal drugs taken under supervision to promote health and the misuse of harmful drugs which endanger health?
      and after the input the children will be asked:
  (3) To what extent they consider that this programme has helped them to avoid taking risks with their own health.
  By finding what the children already know, we hope to extend their knowledge rather than cover old ground and so our intention is that the children will be asked to complete two questionnaires. To

---

preserve confidentiality, another teacher who will not recognise the children's writing will analyse the returns. This means that no-one will know what individual children say. Only the class tallies will be used to plan the programme. A copy of these questionnaires will be in the secretary's office from Monday 20th to Friday 24th November and you are invited to come into school to read them. However, please do not tell your child about the contents in advance! Every child will easily cope with the reading in the questionnaire and the tick box system of replying ensures that everyone can have their say.

If you would prefer that your child did not take part, please inform the secretary, or if you would like further information, please arrange to see Mrs Amos who will be in charge of the project. Thank you for your cooperation.

Yours sincerely

Although this kind of approach involves early preparation and extra organisation, it does allow the researcher to proceed with confidence, knowing that the children's and parents' rights have been respected. The purpose of the research was explained along with some reciprocation, i.e. that a totally relevant programme would be planned.

One sixteen-year-old who left school with no qualifications at all, was asked to complete a lengthy questionnaire about her school experience. The reciprocation offered was that the researchers would use the information to get things better 'for the next cohort of pupils'. She replied, 'I think you's have got a cheek asking me to fill this in after all you should have came and told us what to do for the best instead of asking us lots of things to help other people' (Gow and Macpherson 1984).

I rest my case!

The context

This text is mainly concerned to help teachers carry out small-scale pieces of action research in their own classrooms. These teachers aim to explain the impact of their action plan on a small number of pupils, and so any recording or reporting can take the form of action research case studies. Why, then, is the context so important?

This is because the research question which initiates any change that will be made, has not been conceptualised in the abstract, but in the intimate knowledge of the pupils in the class and the resources which either facilitate or limit that change. As they plan, teachers visualise the possible effects in their own environment. They fully understand that an action plan which would be entirely appropriate in one classroom with one set of pupils and resources, might not be so fortuitous in another. But readers are not party to this thinking, and while some may have a wide range of experience in schools, others will be more limited and find empathising with the innovation difficult. They need details of the rationalisation to let them understand the happenings in that particular context, because it might differ significantly from their own. Providing details helps generalisation.

In a collaborative venture, where several teachers might contemplate the same starting-out idea, they would need to contextualise the idea to suit their own learning environment, e.g. by adapting and amending the research question and judging for themselves the pace at which changes could be introduced. These factors, i.e. those which caused the amendments, are the ones that need to be made explicit in any research report or thesis which is to be read by others, for only through appreciating the research environment can readers fully understand the subtleties of any action plan as it unfolds. Full understanding can only come from 'seeing' the teachers and their children in their own surroundings.

What kind of detail would be appropriate?

Background details for case study action research

Pseudonyms for each child
These protect the identity of the children, keep the text reader-friendly, and make it easier for readers to keep track of each child's responses to the changes which are made.

Age
Knowing the age lets the reader understand the suitability of the action plan, or in any piece of collaborative work, the amendments which were made in each context. For example, the interpretation of 'Play' as a topic and the chosen interventions could be different in the nursery and in each of the first three years of the primary school. Age knowledge also lets readers judge the progress the children make, in relation to the topic, the action plan and possibly developmental norms.

Children's home environment

It *could* be helpful to know if the children were from 'advantaged' or 'disadvantaged' homes, but only if this affected the research action plan. If such descriptions are used, it is best to spell out, in non-judgmental language, what the impact is, e.g. 'As the parents were unable to provide books at home, these ten-year-olds could not have shared reading practice there. As a result, this provision was built into the curriculum so that the children had experience of a paired reading scheme before they themselves became the "experts" helping in the infant class. This delayed any immediate move into the innovation.' Without this information, the pace of change might have been questioned by the reader. Understanding the context also lets the reader appreciate the difficulties the children could have faced, e.g. taking on a new role in an innovation without any experience of the part they had to play.

Details of the school

Inner city, rural, community, denominational? Open plan or traditional? Single or multiple stream? Well resourced? With easy access to libraries? A supportive community? An active P.T.A./School board?

Details of the class

Number of children – proportion of boys:girls? Grouping system – ability/social/varied? Classroom climate – friendly/hostile, ambitious/ non-competitive? Wide range of ability or all at the same level of work? Relationship to those in authority?

These are some of the characteristics which could be useful depending on the reason why the children have been chosen and what the innovation entails. There will be others. No reader however, should have any piece of information which is not directly explaining the research that is underway.

N.B. When writing about the context, only record the information which influences the research. Students, used to writing a context section in their placement folders which has to cover the full curriculum, can be misguided here and write much more than is required. And so it is best to consider each sentence and ask, 'Is this information important to any stage of the actual research plan?' If not, it is best omitted.

Sometimes students in universities anticipating their placement in school, have to plan ahead because their time in school is short and they also have teaching preparation. They are anxious to get the reading done so that they can fully understand their topic and have guidance as to the best ways to implement the research. While this is laudable and understandable, it can cause problems. These can occur if the contextualisation period has been too short, preventing them appreciating all the factors which could make their chosen topic unsuitable in that particular context. Sometimes their original plan can be readily adapted, sometimes not, and in that case, they have to start thinking again. This is why checking the context as early as possible and getting the teacher's approval for any plan is essential.

Example

Amy explained her predicament:

I wanted to introduce peer-assessment for my research, and I had done quite a bit of reading before I went into school, but when I got there the teacher said, 'With this lot? You must be joking – they are far too streetwise, I can just imagine what kinds of things they'd come up with.'

So I needed to start again. I was an observer in the class for a bit and I decided that I needed something to quieten the atmosphere, so that the children would concentrate on their work. The teacher could hold them but I didn't think I could keep them on task. Panic was setting in.

The word 'atmosphere' was the most helpful and so I looked at literature on 'classroom climate'. I couldn't find enough to give me a good review of literature. More panic! Then I thought of my option course in the University, and that was music, and my music tutor thought that playing music in the classroom at certain times could have a calming effect. So I went straight to the music section in the Library. There I found many different kinds of 'music' including tapes of dolphin sounds which made a diversion so that something different was afoot in the classroom. Finding literature was still difficult, but some American texts were helpful and I found articles on the web…

This had been a worrying time for Amy, but by focusing her topic and choosing key words for her literature search, she had found an interesting and worthwhile, even innovative topic for her research. She considered that doing something totally different had helped her build relationships with the children and the fact that it was 'music, and a mixture of kinds', let the children make suggestions and participate in the development. Amy was sure that establishing a positive relationship enabled her to teach with much more confidence, and was anxious to plan other ways of making the classroom different.

Some advice for students

Make contact with your placement school as soon as this is possible and arrange discussion times with your class teacher. Ask for advice on:
- the suitability of your topic for these children in their specific environment;
- any past learning experience which the children have had which might affect your starting-off point;
- any children with particular difficulties in your proposed topic area;
- any children who should not be the focus of your research.

Before visiting school at all, it is a good idea to have a list of written questions, so that they can be left with the teacher if discussion time is curtailed. Having written answers also helps you remember details because your 'talk-time' will have to cover many issues. And if the teacher is not familiar with research in the classroom, a brief written synopsis explaining its purpose and aims would probably be appreciated, and get you off on the right foot! It could also contribute to the introduction in the thesis. Writing things down is rarely wasted.

Afterwards, be sure to make notes about your discussion with the teacher and keep them to hand. Let the teacher see that you value the advice that was given.

CHAPTER 4

Gathering data

The research question has been formulated, the texts are read for now, and all the pitfalls have been considered. The critical question now becomes, 'What action(s) can I take to gather evidence to answer the research question?', for you will remember that only data which does that job can be used. Gathering other information which is fascinating and might come in handy in another investigation can be sorely tempting, but if it is extraneous to the main thrust of the enquiry, it only serves to confuse the main issue and is best forgotten.

What kind of action plan will be best? If the research question is planned according to the format suggested on p.14, it will begin 'If I (do this)' and this may suggest the kinds of action which could be appropriate to gather the most relevant data. Identifying the implicit hypotheses within a research question (see p.38) helps determine the categories which have to be monitored if they are to form the key to the data analysis. The literature may also have held useful cues. The extent of any action plan will depend on the amount of time the researcher has available, the number of subjects taking part and whether the respondents are all in school or whether waiting time for replies from parents has to be built in to the plan. Moreover, each investigation will have its own implicit time span, i.e. the length of time that any change to improve the status quo could reasonably be expected to take.

It is best to build research times into the teaching forward plan, because then the most appropriate slots can be set aside and the implications for both the research and the other curriculum areas can be considered together. This time-tabling is especially helpful for student teachers who sometimes find it difficult to hold on to their research time if they are asked to cover other duties. It is also sensible to consider factors like the weather, e.g. how easy will it be to make outdoor observations of motor skills when the children are muffled up in January? Or if the 'bug' strikes, is there time to make up lost ground?

As you can see, there are lots of organisational issues and these will vary depending on the parameters of the action plan, but the following questions need to be considered.

- What?
- How?
- When?
- Where?
- With whom?

- What resources?
- What recordings will be made?
- What implications?
- Who needs to be informed?
- Will these actions provide evidence to answer the research question?

What? What will the investigation cover? One whole curriculum area or just one aspect, e.g. listening? A thematic study or a cross-curricular project? If the latter, can you assume that transfer of learning will occur? If not, what will you do? What information from the literature is guiding the planning of the research?

How? How will you gather the data? What data gathering strategies will bring in the kind of evidence you need? How do you plan to reduce bias? How will you set up triangulation? Will the children know they are taking part in research? What are the implications if they do and if they do not?

When? Once a week or more often? At the same time each day? (Consider the possibilities of the children being tired or restless). For how many weeks? Are any other school plans likely to impinge on this time? If so, is there an alternative spot?

Where? In the classroom or in a quiet area, in the hall or out of doors? (Consider the implication of moving the pupils and any organisation.) Are there 'distractions' e.g. parents coming to collect children in another class, school dinners being set up in the hall or the learning support teacher requiring 'your' space? Is there a plug for a tape recorder and is the space quiet enough to allow recordings to be heard?

With whom? What children will participate and how will they be selected? Will other adults be involved, perhaps to share observation sessions or to cover the non-research children? Remember to remind them in advance of the times – and thank them afterwards! Will parents be needed or others in the community? How will they be approached and selected? Will they be willing to take part? What if they aren't? How will that affect your sample?

What resources? Is the equipment such as video, tape recorder, computers or language centre available at the right times? Is the microphone sufficiently strong to record the children's voices from the necessary distance? Will questionnaires/interview or observation schedules need to be prepared in advance? Are some to be posted home or trusted to the children? Is there a box in a secure place for the completed, anonymous questionnaires?

N.B. Always check the reliability of the equipment, and practise using it to avoid disaster on the day.

What recordings will be made? Field notes – where, when and how much detail will need to be recorded? Observation schedules – how many, what format and what about non-verbal behaviour? Questionnaires – how many questions and how many respondents? Does anyone in authority need to check the questions? Who needs to see the answers? How is the data to be analysed?

What implications? If the findings point to other things being required or certain changes needing to be made, is the climate such that they can happen? If not, what will you do?

Who needs to be informed? Do parents need to give permission? Does any child with a special need require to be catered for? Does any 'outside' body e.g. Advisors, Board of Governors, PTA groups, need to give permission or would it be a courtesy to let them know the research plan? And last but most important of all:

Will this action provide enough 'objective' evidence to allow you to answer the research question and show that you can justify the claims you make?
N.B. If some children are not involved in the research, their time needs to be planned too. They need absorbing, useful activities to save them wasting time and possibly being resentful or disruptive.

The action itself may be preceded by an information gathering exercise, perhaps to find the level of the children's work or their pre-action knowledge about the research topic or to see what kinds of activities they would like to do. In similar vein, information may be gathered after the research to find pupils' views on having been involved. But these pre and post action strategies do not make up the total action plan, for that is a carefully planned series of actions taken to improve a situation, not only an information gathering activity.

Carr and Kemmis (1986) affirm this differentiation between ethnographic research and classroom action research. They explain:

> Action research aims at improvement in three areas: first the improvement of a practice; second the improvement of understanding of the practice by its practitioners; and third the improvement of the situation in which the practice takes place. The aim of involvement stands shoulder to shoulder with the aims of improvement.

So action researchers are not flies on the wall but are in there, fully involved in making and monitoring and evaluating the change.

Data gathering instruments

1. Field notes
2. Audio and videotape recording
3. Structured observation schedules
4. Questionnaires
5. Interviews.

Field notes

This is a quick and unobtrusive way of recording aspects of behaviour as they occur or as soon as is practical afterwards. The notes are quick observations of something that is happening now, and so they have a liveliness and authenticity that is pleasing. They may record usual behaviours – perhaps teachers are concerned that a child's repertoire of skills is limited and wish to gather evidence of the various competences the child usually displays to affirm or deny their gut feelings. On the other hand, one-off incidents can be fascinating too, for surprises can cause teachers to reconsider their earlier judgments. The recordings can be incidental, looking to build a general picture of the child's participation, or they can be pre-planned, the observer only looking for specific incidents, e.g. how the child's fine motor control was manifest in writing, drawing, threading and painting.

Many nurseries have a sticky label system. Each teacher or nursery nurse has responsibility for observing a small number of children and over a week perhaps, will ensure that recordings cover all aspects of development: intellectual, social, emotional, physical and motor. Each day the labels go into a notebook and the teachers meet weekly to discuss the emerging picture of each child. The resulting case study, which comes from a bank of field notes amassed over time, provides a wealth of material which can then be used as evidence for pupil profiling. The recordings show developmental trends as well as areas and times of progress and regression. What they do not do is offer any explanation of the reason why these things occurred. If the teacher suspects that there is a 'home cause' or a 'peer crisis cause', then this can be added later, but the recordings should just describe the incident rather than try to explain why, for this could be based on speculation – not a good research tool!

The main difficulty is that these recordings can be highly subjective, with some observations made and not others. Furthermore, those that *are* made may depend on the individual preference, or the skill, even the professionalism, of the recorder. To try to overcome this, each teacher can observe different children each week, and differences noted in observations can be made the focus of discussion. And so the notes shouldn't be too brief because some incidents will need to be recalled at that time.

Field notes can also be used to record all kinds of incidents in teaching and learning, e.g. what certain pupils contribute in cooperative group work. Student teachers may also find it useful to start with a blank slate and record incidents that seem to explain e.g. what experienced teachers do to make the day proceed smoothly, for perhaps they do this automatically with no explanation, and the students are left wondering why it doesn't happen for them.

And so field notes have many uses (see Figure 4.1) and studying them can certainly throw up new ideas for further research.

Field Notes	
Advantages	**Disadvantages**
A straightforward personal record	May record too much – obscuring main focus
Useful for specific observations which can show a lot of detail	Can be very subjective
Comparisons over time are easily made	No use for conversations
Very good way of collecting preliminary material for a case study	Must be analysed immediately to allow recall of detail

Figure 4.1　The advantages and disadvantages of field notes

Audio and videotape recording

One of the things field notes cannot do is to record conversations and here the audiotape recorder comes into its own, for if it is placed near the children, it can record spaces in interactions, silences, phatics, speed of diction and voice intonation as well as the actual words that are spoken. This is important if the real meaning within any interaction is to be clear, because the actual words only carry ten per cent! (Argyle 1960). If this is so, then recording and interpreting all the aspects together must be a good way of reducing bias.

Video recording further helps these analyses, as body postures and facial expressions can portray reactions and subsequent actions, but these can be misleading, and need confirming evidence such as that gained through triangulation (see assessing attitudes p.73). Another difficulty is that in making these close-up recordings, procedural bias, i.e. the children's reactions being affected by the research procedure, is very likely to come into play. A zoom lens and a camera tripod can help.

If whole body movements are to be recorded, video is the only realistic tool, because not many people are expert enough to use Laban notation, or any other movement recording system which uses a stave like music and on which the detail of movement can be scribed. If anyone did wish to use this, and if the record was to be part of a thesis, the candidate would have to check that the examiner could interpret these movement scores.

Video, of course, is not just for movement. It can record friendship patterns, group work interactions or any aspect of teaching. The recording can be analysed later by several people and this is a real bias-reducing bonus. However, the difficulty of getting exactly the right thing on tape needs to be considered. If the camera is set up in the classroom or playground and left to run (so that the place is as natural as can be), you can be sure that the most relevant happening occurs just beyond the camera's range! To prevent this, any helper-recorders have to know exactly what you are after and they have to have the skill to see it happening, even through the eyepiece of the camera. This needs lots of practice. Piloting before the main event is as essential as checking out that the camera really does work in that socket, that it has that the capacity to zoom in and capture the essence of whatever is being studied, and that the film is fresh enough to record the colour and the spirit of the day.

With both audio and video recording, background noise is a real bugbear and can make transcribing conversations really difficult. And yet if you take the children to a different, quieter place, procedural bias looms! What can be done? Some dry runs to familiarise the children with the procedures in the new place is a good idea, but then you could be accused of hogging the equipment or wasting resources. So once more, detailed forward planning is the key to success, for then you will be able to defend your plan. Remember to check whether parents need to be informed too.

Pros and cons of using audio and video recording are summarised in Figure 4.2.

Structured observation schedules

Observation, i.e. being able to see rather than just looking, is a critically important skill in teaching. This is because it is the basis of being able to understand and act upon all the complexities in the classroom, e.g. how and why different children respond to different teaching episodes and therefore what to do next; how peer pressures may influence children's

Audio and video tape	
Advantages	**Disadvantages**
Makes accurate record, may be replayed often	Procedure bias (presence of equipment/moving children)
Gives more detail than other records	Background noise/movement may be distracting
Records as researcher does something else, no personal bias	Video needs someone to film moving incidents
Can be transcribed later or at home	Time consuming to transcribe NB Examiner may not have time or opportunity to listen/view original

Figure 4.2 The advantages and disadvantages of audio and videotape recording

progress and therefore what kind of grouping would be best; what specific problems some children face and what resources can be used to help. Many important decisions rest on the teacher's observational skills. But good observation needs practice. Most teachers would say that it is 'a developing skill', and few would claim to be expert in all teaching situations. And so two teachers embarking on data gathering which uses an observation schedule to record classroom happenings can act as partners – one developing observation skills, the other the teaching competency which has been selected. In this scenario, the teachers need to have a sound, non-competitive, reciprocal working relationship. If trust and possibly confidentiality have been assured, then this kind of peer appraisal can work, especially if ground rules are established and obeyed.

If the research can be viewed in this light, i.e. as a partnership, where both participants are gathering data together, each aware of the difficult role the other has, the enterprise can benefit both, for both will be extending their skills. This is much more fruitful than regarding observation as a threat where one watches the other teach and notes 'things that go wrong'.

Of course, when students and teachers work together, it is not realistic to suggest that they could be equal partners, but if the students can appreciate what is involved in making sound 'objective' observations (i.e. the skill as well as the time that is involved), this might just prevent them becoming so tied up in their own role that they take the other for granted, a quite common stance which could jeopardise any chance of collaboration.

Observation schedules are a very useful means of gathering objective data in the classroom. They can be used in different ways, to record aspects of both teaching and learning. The recordings can tell 'when' and 'where' as well as 'how often' and so provide a rich source of information for reflection and evaluation. They can form the basis of discussions and forward planning, and even be used to justify requests for resources or extra classroom help. This is because having evidence puts the applicant in a much stronger position. Moreover, several schedules spaced sequentially through a series of teaching episodes can show the progress that is being made, and even prove that 'imposed' innovations do or do not work in that particular classroom. They can identify the highs and the lows and cause the researchers to pause and wonder why; they can even prompt changes in the process of the action plan.

Of course, if this is to happen, the schedule, like any other data gathering instrument, must be carefully designed. The key words are appropriateness, clarity and brevity:

- appropriateness, because the recordings must provide data to take thinking in that key area forward;
- clarity, because the observer must be able to identify exactly what is to be recorded;
- brevity, because with children moving here and there, it is very difficult to 'see' more than one or two things!

Selecting classroom subjects

If the purpose of the research is to monitor and evaluate the effects of the research action on specific pupils, and remember it is planned to provide some kind of improved learning environment for them, then these pupils are the research subjects. This could be 'all the pupils in primary 3', or it could be just one group of three or four children who would benefit from some remedial or extension input. If this is the case, the research report will probably be in the form of several case studies. These will give a great deal of detail about each stage of the process and the individual children's reactions to it. The report would say, 'As a result of (this action), this was discovered for these children in this context.'

If only a few children are involved, the possibility of generalisation, i.e. spreading and sharing the findings in the hope that they will be applicable and useful to many more children, seems remote. In fact, researchers are best to disclaim automatic generalisation to a wider population. However, if they share details of the context and the personnel and the planning of their research, then readers can extract parts of the report which were similar to their own situation. This makes generalisation a much more serious possibility.

But perhaps the teacher-researchers wished to monitor their own competence in an aspect of classroom life, e.g. developing their discussion skills? Who will be chosen as subjects then? If the chosen children are already reliable and imaginative respondents, how will the teachers discern whether the efforts that have been made have been of benefit? Alternatively, selecting children who have difficulty in talking out could skew the findings the other way, because helping them develop their skills could take longer than should result from the teacher's new level of competence. And so a larger, randomly selected group (every fourth name on the register across two classes?) could be the fairest way to measure the impact of the research. Or perhaps a group of children drawn from each of the different ability groups in the class? But then the effect of the more able on the less able would need to be considered, for in a true discussion, the teacher is not going to be able to direct questions at reluctant talkers and the articulate children are likely to dominate. Can you see how the selection of the research subjects can lead to a charge of biased results?

Designing the schedule

Before the schedule is designed, the observer and the teacher need to set some ground rules so that each understands the other's remit and doesn't inadvertently hamper or intrude. At the planning stage, joint decisions need to cover:
- the aspect and detail of teaching or learning that has to be observed;
- the length and timing of each observation;
- where the observer has to be in relation to the action;
- whether the observer should interact in any way or stay quietly observing;
- what any inquisitive children, who ask what the observer is doing, are to be told;
- when the feedback discussion will take place.

There needs to be agreement about the aspect and detail of what has to be observed. The following example concerns the topic 'Asking questions' and these might be the discussion points on what has to be recorded:
- Questions to all children or a nominated few? (Can they sit near each other to ease observation or would this highlight that certain children were being targeted?)
- Closed and factual recall questions or only higher order questions? (Has the actual wording to be incorporated or is it enough to say that a higher order question was used?)

- Do the teacher and the observer have a shared understanding of what a higher order question is?
- Have the children's replies to be recorded as a back-up to the tape recording, which can be difficult to hear?
- What other mechanisms have to be recorded? (Phatics, pauses, silences?)
- What about non-verbal communication? (Nods, frowns, smiles, moving towards the speaker?)
- What about the distribution of questions? (Is it important if one child is swamped?)
- Will the topic or learning activity encourage/inhibit the children being studied? Could this bias the recording? (Are there enough different topics for the children to reply easily and confidently in some, if not all?)
- Should the tone of voice be recorded as an enabling/inhibiting strategy? (If so, how is this to be done?)
- What about the feedback which the teacher gives to the replying child? Should this be recorded? (The feedback might stop a child answering again or inhibit another!)

As you can see from this list there are many issues which need to be considered, and in a more complex scenario, perhaps introducing something new to the class, there will be even more. This is quite different from a teacher drawing out a schedule and asking an observer to 'record what you see'.

Two examples of teachers using observation schedules in this collaborative, prepared way follow. Karen, with Jim as a mentor, used this data gathering strategy to help with her classroom interaction. She had felt deskilled when she had difficulty in introducing an integrated day type of classroom organisation. Tony used another to assess his children's developing competence in discussion. He added another dimension by using one child in each group as recorder.

Example 1. Topic: Positive communication. Teacher: Karen. Class: Primary 2

Karen explains

I had just managed to organise my class into an integrated day so that I could have time to work with individual groups. I felt this was necessary as there was a wide range of ability in the class, and apart from that, the once a year entry into school meant that some children were nearly a year older than others. In our smallish school there was no learning support for children in the infant classes. We just had to cope as well as we could.

The teacher in the next bay, Jim, had the integrated day up and running and it was working well. All the children were busy all of the time and he had time to work with groups or individuals whenever this was necessary. I had expected my class to settle and do the same, but the new organisation made me very tense. You know what it is like trying to juggle all the balls in the air and cope with the early finishers. Some of the children didn't feel confident in moving from one activity to another without instruction and others just didn't seem to be able to remember what to do next despite all the charts I had made. It was totally exhausting.

Eventually, because the atmosphere in my class had changed, I asked Jim for advice. I didn't fancy this at all and thought that if he was patronising, I'd freak. He was more experienced but still young, so he could sympathise with my problems and when he told me about his first two years and the difficulties he'd had, I realised he genuinely wanted to help. At first, he listened 'over the wall' because his bay was next door, and he said it appeared that the organisation had taken over and I had turned into a nag! Of course he didn't say these exact words, but he suggested that I could be much more positive and try to make the day fun.

It was hard realising that I needed to make more changes because I had worked so hard, but in my head I knew that I had to stop saying 'Don't do that,' or 'Does nobody remember to read the chart,' or 'Why is no-one putting their work in the basket?' I could hear myself, but I couldn't stop. So we agreed to try the observation schedule to see if I could make the day much more positive and friendly and to see what effect this had on my three groups.

Before the observation of my teaching began, I tried to recall incidents which I could have handled better and tried to think of more positive ways of coping. Jim took time to observe the children just so that he could be sure of recording the correct names. He knew the children by sight, but not all their names or which groups they were in. We needed some time to prepare the observation schedule and decide where the observer would sit and what he should say if the children asked what he was doing. We also thought that Jim being in the class before the research actually

> happened was a way of reducing bias because everything would be more natural if there were no new faces! The other teachers began to wonder what was afoot but we just said we were preparing some team teaching which was true – well nearly! We had explained our idea to the head teacher who was delighted and she took Jim's class for the half hour observation sessions. We did the analysis together after the children left – being infant teachers, we had time in school and the usual preparation went home.

Karen and Jim prepared the schedule to suit their particular time frame i.e. knowing that they had 30 minutes per day when they could concentrate on their research. They decided to have one session early in the day when 'it was easier to hang on to the prepared comments' and another the following day just before lunch when 'the children are usually restless and there is all the tidying up to be done, and coats and shoes have to be coped with'. And because they decided that only Karen's side of the

Topic: Communication						
		Positive Verbal	*Positive N. V.*	*Negative Verbal*	*Negative N.V.*	
Group	1	✓✓✓	O ✓✓ Anne			Tuesday 9.15-9.45 Recording 9.30-9.45
	2	✓✓	✓ ✓O Graeme	✗		
	3	O ③ Sacha		✗ ✓✓ Colin	✗ Colin	
Group	1	✓ ② Peter	✓ O		✓	11.45-12.15 Recording 12.00-12.15
	2	✓ O O Lyn	✓✓	O O O O Colin Ian	✓ ✓ ✓	
	3	✓ ① Jane		✓✓	✗ ✗ ✗ ✗ Colin Colin Alan Colin	

✓	General
✗	Repetition of same instruction (negative)
O	Good effort – remember this – e.g.
①	'You organised the painting well yesterday, see if you can do it again.'
②	'Everyone has finished because there has been no time wasting.'
③	'It's great to know how well you can plan your time chart.'

Figure 4.3   Observation schedule (Karen)

interaction was to be recorded, they could subdivide the schedule by class groups. Jim's familiarisation time in the classroom, ahead of the actual recording time, helped ensure that he got the recording of individual names correct. This pattern was repeated four times.

Jim found that he could quickly record the detail of some of the most positive interactions (see Figure 4.3) and in the feedback session he could remember how the children reacted, although this had not been part of his original remit. Karen explained later how this boosted her confidence. What the teachers had not anticipated and what turned out to be a real bonus was that the pattern of interaction towards the different groups emerged. Group three were having a poor time of it largely because of Colin and so Karen resolved to find more ways of interacting positively with that group. Her next aim was to think about non-verbal communication so that her pupils were not confused by having conflicting messages.

Example 2. Topic: Improving discussion. Teacher: Tony. Class: Secondary 2

Tony explains
> The observation schedule I used was really a prompt to make the children say something in discussion groups. As you know, oral work is part of the accreditation system now and so the children have to practise speaking to their peers. Before I embarked on book reviews, I wanted them to gain confidence in speaking in a small group. This class was newly formed from several Year 2 groups and I was new to them too, but I hadn't expected the children to be so constrained. My idea was to arrange them in groups and set them a discussion topic. We had been talking about characters in a teenage novel, Discovery by Pete Johnston, and I thought that their own experience would let them say what they thought about each character's behaviour. They seemed keen to do this but when they went into groups they didn't have much to say, and when I went near to listen they clammed up or at best asked me questions so that we had a teacher → pupil dialogue.
>
> And so I explained that the point of a discussion was that they should speak among themselves and that they should ask each other questions, or ask for explanations or put forward arguments. I then told them that one person in each group was to be a recorder and that the recording would show who had spoken and to whom.

The children knew that it was just turns that counted – they didn't have to say anything special. I was just measuring quantity of talk at this point and so everyone was quite relaxed. The pupils enjoyed this and became quite voluble, especially when the recorders got it wrong. They soon realised that recording was difficult if they all spoke at once and this began to establish some order in the groups. They all wanted arrows going to their name! (See Figure 4.4.)

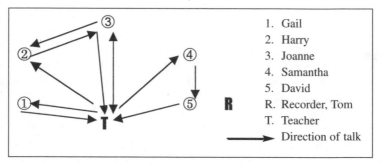

1. Gail
2. Harry
3. Joanne
4. Samantha
5. David
R. Recorder, Tom
T. Teacher
———→ Direction of talk

Figure 4.4 Observation schedule (Tony)

After a bit the schedules became messy but they got the talk going – or perhaps it was because I had promised not to listen in! After one or two turns at this, I asked each group to summarise their discussion, and each child had to relay one sentence back to the class. This was in terms of what the group had found, rather than any personal viewpoint, and this eased them into talking out.

And so the pupils gained some confidence. Although it was a long way from giving individual book reviews to the whole class, it was a start. The recording took away some of the pressure, and when I heard one of the groups talking about 'our research', I was quite pleased.

And so it can be seen that observation schedules can be used in different ways – even when there is no teacher free to help out. The main thing is that the schedules produce objective evidence of carefully planned changes.

To ensure clarity in recording and later in reporting, the information alongside the schedule should include:
- the topic being observed;
- the specific items to be recorded;

- the subjects – pupils/observer/recorder;
- teacher;
- details of the coding used;
- the time and place.

This done, the schedules can be easily recalled at the time when the data has to be analysed.

Observing and assessing attitudes

Often teachers say that they wish to assess their pupils' attitudes to their work, especially if they wish to monitor any change in attitude over time. They seem reluctant to agree that it would be 'safer' or more objective to record the patterns of behaviour which were, in fact, the evidence of changed attitudes. They tell me, 'I'd be a funny kind of teacher if I didn't know whether — was lazy or not,' or 'Alright, he'll maybe do a bit more work but if he is still aggressive and cheeky, there hasn't been any attitude change, has there?' It is a difficult problem, not helped by some parents' views that their child's poor attitude must be the teacher's fault.

However, it is very easy to make mistakes about attitudes, and it is better to provide evidence to substantiate claims. I remember one devastated girl who bitterly resented being told she was lazy. The teacher, who had intended the comment to mean that the girl had more ability than was being shown (and how would she know that?), had not thought that she would react in this way and, as a result, the relationship and the workload never recovered. And so it is best to omit comments like 'He is bored stiff' and talk about the child's reluctance to join in or whatever it was that indicated his boredom in the first place. It is fatally easy to misinterpret facial expressions and body postures (as in Figure 4.5). Take care!

Figure 4.5   Motivating Martin

Observation schedules	
Advantages	**Disadvantages**
Records behaviours which are important for data analysis	Can be difficult to 'catch' transitory moves
A considerable amount of specific information can be gathered	Much information is lost, e.g. non-verbals, pauses
The schedule gives a strong visual impact – problems stand out	The observer is obviously making notes – procedural bias

Figure 4.6   The advantages and disadvantages of observation schedules

In summary, Figure 4.6 shows the pros and cons of observation schedules.

Questionnaires

The questionnaire is a survey of different opinions from (usually) large numbers of people who provide anonymous replies. The questions are standardised, i.e. each respondent receives the same number and kind. The respondents are 'a random selection' chosen by sampling, e.g. every fourth name on the voters' roll, and this is one way of reducing bias. Some bias can remain however, due to an imbalance in the replies. If, for example, a disproportionate group of unemployed people or too busy people or uninterested people do not reply, the sample will be distorted. Questionnaires may also be used in schools or even within classes, wherever 'anonymous' responses are the best ways of getting at the truth, for example, finding how many children completed their homework on time and without assistance! And once anonymity has been promised, steps have to be taken to reassure the children or the other teachers or the parents that, even in a small community, this *can* happen. No names, no home details which could identify, ticking boxes rather than handwriting, a safe but outside the classroom collection point, all of these details need attention. And of course the claims made from the findings must be directly related to the size of the sample which took part, as well as the questions that were asked.

The questionnaire then, is a quick and effective way of gathering a lot of information from a number of people – quick, that is, once the questions have been finalised and effective if the answers produce helpful responses. Although inexperienced researchers may think this data gathering strategy is relatively straightforward, just 'asking some questions and comparing the replies', it can be really difficult to conceptualise questions which are clear and unambiguous, which enable the respondents to reply 'honestly' and which are free of contamination, i.e. the response to one question having a knock-on effect and influencing another. But these are the criteria which must be met if the questionnaire is to be a credible data gathering strategy.

How then can researchers ensure that their questions are clear to all their respondents? First, they must answer the question: 'What exactly, do I want to find out?' and this can be harder than at first appears. The next step is to focus on, then analyse each concept within the question. This example will try to show how.

Example. Topic: Lifestyle and fitness in children
'I want to find if children who walk to school are fitter than those who come by car or bus.'

At first glance, this would seem a straightforward enough investigation. A questionnaire entry could ask the children, 'How do you travel to school?' and then each child's reply could be compared to the results of a fitness test. The riddle is solved! Or is it? Let's look at the question again. Consider first, the distance the children walk. Are children who live just by the school entitled to tick the box which asks if they walk to school, or does the distance need to be qualified? If so, do the children appreciate 'length' in the abstract or does this have to be spelled out? And if so, how would this be done?
N.B. It is essential to consider the knowledge base of the respondents. Will they have the conceptual understanding to reply?
Then the concept of fitness has to be considered. Are the children recorded as being fit if they can run round the school twice or is some cardiovascular measurement envisaged? If so, is the equipment available and in a 'measurement' of this kind, do the parents need to give permission? Another critical query is whether the walk to school impacts on fitness at all, and of course this can only be claimed if regularity of walking is considered alongside the distance that has to be covered. Does walking once per week or twice or every day over several weeks 'count' the same? If it is important to differentiate between responses, and in this example it would be, then the question needs to incorporate a sliding scale to allow the different inputs to be shown.

And what about the children's other activities? Perhaps they impact on fitness more than walking to school does, especially if the walk is a leisurely stroll chatting to friends! And so, do 'speed' and 'regularity' need to complement 'distance' in the questions the children are asked?

Furthermore, the other activities the children do, make a significant contribution to fitness, do they not? It could be important to find what they were, especially if they made a different kind of contribution, e.g. strength or mobility. How would basketball compare to ballet as a fitness enhancer do you think? Would it be important to consider these differences? Or if this proved too difficult, would you just select children who walked to school but did not participate in other forms of exercise as your sample? You would need to make this clear so that the research findings could be interpreted in context.

As you can see, all the concepts within a question have to be unpicked and the relevant variables included in the questionnaire, for if they are ignored they could badly bias the results. This process has a hidden bonus for it also indicates the types of questions which can most usefully feature in the questionnaire.

N.B. Remember that the researcher is not present as the questionnaire is being completed. The questions must stand alone. It is therefore best to replace difficult terminology with easier phrases – or if this is not possible, to give an example to clarify what is meant, for if the respondents are not clear what the answer entails, they will either put in their own interpretation or leave the answer blank. And if they have to constantly wonder, 'What does this mean?' they may well abandon answering at all, because there is no compulsion for them to do so, is there?

As you read this you may think, 'Ah, but in my class I can go round and sort things out for the children.' Yes, you can, but what about confidentiality? And bias? Surely these important research principles will have been lost, for children, knowing that you know them, are likely to aim to please – or to shock. You certainly would have less chance of an 'honest' reply. Perhaps if this, i.e. an interactive way of gathering data, is more suitable in your particular situation, you should choose to interview the respondents, because this method allows you to probe and prompt and explain. The strategy must be chosen in the light of the competence and experience of the respondents.

N.B. A word of caution earlier urged you to consider the children's knowledge base as you compiled questions. A similar word asks you to make sure of your own! If you wished to investigate a complex issue, if for example, you wanted to find out about the celebrations of different religious groups so that you could acknowledge these in your classroom, you have to be sure that you know enough to be able to compile a questionnaire which did not offend some groups or even 'let you down' in the eyes of the recipients. If you feel unsure, perhaps arrange a face to face meeting with one or two knowledgeable people first. They can advise and the collaboration can enrich the subsequent questionnaire by suggesting more pertinent questions.

One of the main disadvantages of a questionnaire is that although people answer your questions, there is not usually the room for them to tell you the reasoning behind their response. If, for example, you asked the children to list their favourite school activities with the best one at the top, you would find that ten of the children liked playtime best, but they wouldn't tell you why. This is called data degradation, i.e. loss of potential information. To overcome this you may have asked the children to write their reasons and provided time and space for them to comply. However, many children find writing explanations very difficult. Certainly it is time-consuming, and the researcher has to weigh up the pros of this against the loss of other answers and in the knowledge that analysing data from 'open' replies can be perplexing unless the categories are clearly defined.

This brings us to the different types of questions which can usefully be included in a questionnaire. Some are easier to answer, some need considerable thought. The respondents have to be kept interested and keen to complete the questionnaire so that the responses can provide the most comprehensive data. Let's consider this issue now.

Questions as items in the questionnaire
Different kinds of question add interest, give variety and help to prevent the respondents from replying without reading the question carefully. The design of each question will also affect the kind of response which is given, so it is useful to try to anticipate the amount of detail which is required from each question to give you the data you require. The following are 'closed questions', i.e. those having a Yes/No answer:

Do you agree with school uniform? Yes   No   Don't know
                                    ❏   ❏   ❏
                                                 Please tick

Then there are closed questions with alternatives, e.g.:
How do you travel to school? Bus   Car   Walk   Train Bicycle
                              ❏   ❏   ❏   ❏   ❏
                                                          Please tick

Closed questions with some scale might be:
What do you think of corporal
punishment?   Approve   Neutral   Disapprove
                         ❏   ❏   ❏
                                                       Please tick

How much of the lesson did
you enjoy?   All of it   Some of it   None of it
                                        ❏   ❏   ❏
                                                                   Please tick

Did you find the work   Too difficult   Just right   Too easy
                                        ❏   ❏   ❏
                                                                   Please tick

There are also closed questions with alternative suggestions e.g.:
Please indicate (1,2,3) the three kinds of class activity which you consider
to be most helpful and the most enjoyable for you.

	helpful (1,2,3)	enjoyable (1,2,3)
having notes dictated by the teacher	❏	❏
having 'stations' and tasks	❏	❏
having debates and discussion groups	❏	❏
doing written examples	❏	❏
researching topics in class	❏	❏
researching topics outside school	❏	❏
using listening posts	❏	❏
using video tapes	❏	❏
other? Please say what.................................	❏	❏

The following are open questions:
What do you think of......?
Please write a few lines about......?

Closed questions can usually be answered quickly because no
explanation is required. Open questions provide more qualitative
information because the respondents are able to express their feelings in
their own words.

There are also cartoon type questions as shown below and in Figure 4.7:
Put a ring around Ralph the Tortoise to show how you feel, when it is time
to do PE.

Several lines of Ralph, or Snoopy or a smiley face, can allow the pupils
to record their evaluation about different aspects of any school
experience. The light-hearted approach is to help them record their true
feelings – thus reducing bias. A sliding scale, recording different feelings,
is implicit in the drawings.

Figure 4.7   Ralph the tortoise

Personal questions
Some questionnaires begin with personal questions, the researchers believing that as their respondents know the answers, they will be able to make a confident start and thus be encouraged to complete the other questions. Others believe these questions are best left last in case they cause offence, e.g. asking for age! Perhaps the best idea is to consider the range of respondents. Schoolchildren won't mind telling you their age while older people could be annoyed especially if the title of the questionnaire didn't indicate the point of your knowing. Even with items like gender, ask yourself, 'Is it important? What use will I make of this information?' for having unnecessary questions wastes space, quite apart from irritating the respondents. One group, asked to fill in a questionnaire immediately after a swimming lesson, were amazed to be asked what sex they were. Of course the student couldn't analyse the data there and then, but a little forethought might just have avoided this somewhat embarrassing situation when one swimmer asked if he couldn't tell!

And so always ask, 'Why do I need to know this?' and if the information won't form part of your analysis, consider the effect of deleting the question.

First impressions
The questionnaire should be attractive, clearly set out, with a title, on crisp paper. This lets the respondents see that the document is important and that you have taken care in considering the design.

Organisation: distribution and collection
'Getting them out and in' needs careful planning too. The following points can help.
  • Include a s.a.e. with a first class stamp in any postal questionnaire. This communicates a sense of urgency and hopefully prevents the document being forgotten. Pupils may deliver them home, but may need several reminders and the condition of the questionnaire after it has been at the bottom of a schoolbag may not be as pristine as might be hoped.

- How many should be sent out? Knowing the population and the importance of the questionnaire may give the researcher some idea of possible waste. A 60 per cent return is reasonable. The number of returns is important for the credibility of claims which may be made.
- How long should respondents have for completing and returning the questionnaires? Usually ten days is a favourable time span, i.e. long enough for very busy but willing respondents and not long enough for the questionnaire to be lost. Postal ones are obviously more costly than pupil dependent ones but they may be safer.
- Timing of distribution. If you have a measure of flexibility, considering the lifestyle of the recipients can influence the return rate. 'Just before the summer holidays' might suit the researcher anticipating a bit of free time for analysis, but holiday preparations might prevent some people replying. Similarly 'just before Christmas' should be avoided if at all possible. Another tense time could be when school reports have just gone home. Disappointed parents may not be feeling too cooperative and so it would be better to wait, especially if questions about the curriculum or the effects of changing organisation are to be asked. The timing could certainly bias the results!
- Collection point. A box in the secretary's office is a good place for anonymous returns to be safely collected. Respondents should not have to hand their 'confidential' replies to anyone connected with the research.

Piloting

Once the questions have been formulated, the most helpful way forward is to pilot the questionnaire on just a small group of people who will be fair but critical, watch as they answer, then study their replies. Watching these first samplers complete the questionnaire can show whether they have readily understood all the questions or indicate the ones causing difficulty. The time taken to complete the questionnaire is important too, for this could indicate that there were too many questions or too few, while studying the responses later shows whether the questions have been interpreted in unexpected ways.

It is usually very revealing if researchers can study several completed questionnaires at the same time, for the similarities and contrasts which emerge immediately indicate the quality and quantity of information which is likely to be collected in the full-scale investigation. At this point there is still time for other questions to be added, unsatisfactory ones to be amended or deleted, or for the balance of open or closed questions to be changed. All researchers must expect to have more than one redraft of questions, always keeping in mind that as the questions change, so might the balance of different kinds of question. So try to replace like with like. The formulation of 'good' questions, the piloting and the early evaluation is time-consuming, but invariably time well spent, for nothing can be more frustrating than realising, too late, that other questions would have provided more significant or relevant answers.

Students often wail, 'Why did they tell me that?', only to discover on rereading their question, the exact reason why, i.e. because 'that' was a legitimate answer to the question they had asked! Figure 4.8 presents a process of developing viable questions.

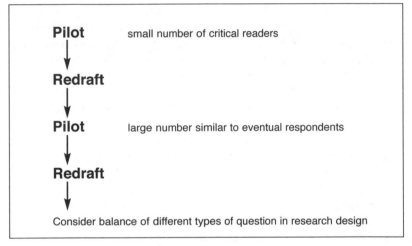

Figure 4.8   Piloting and redrafting questions

It can be helpful for the researcher to compile a questionnaire and then leave it aside for some time – later it can be reread with fresh eyes and from the (imaginary) viewpoint of different recipients, e.g. a newly redundant father, a single parent, a 'well-off' family, someone with reading difficulties, i.e. a representative sample from the population that will receive the questionnaire. This decentring can help the researcher to evaluate the clarity and the balance of the questionnaire from a range of different perspectives. This is important because the researcher will not be at hand to explain at the time the questionnaires are completed.

Sampling

How are the respondents to be selected?

The first question to consider is 'Who are the people who will be affected by the results?', and these, listed, form your research population. The second is, 'How many of these *can* be consulted – in terms of time, cost and availability?' Dividing the possible number by the resource number will give you the sample number. Then you have to decide how that number of people can be randomly selected from the whole research population.

Munn and Drever (1990) tell of two important principles of random sampling:

- each member of the population must have an equal chance of being selected, and
- the chances of one being selected must be quite independent of any other.

One factor which might concern you is willingness! Is there any point sending a questionnaire to a home where you suspect it will be put in the bin, or indeed where the recipients might not be able to read the contents? To have a genuine random sample however, you need to work from a list and take every 6th or 7th or 10th entry, i.e. whatever number has been arithmetically decided by the earlier division, ignoring any inside knowledge of the subjects that you have. After all, you can't know them all and you may be wrong! What you can do is to distribute 'enough' questionnaires so that any non-returns still leave you with sufficient replies to make your claims valid.

Example

If, for example, the school wanted an up-to-date report of parents' views on whether school uniform should be worn, then all the parents form the research population. They are the people affected by the results. Whether the random selection was the parents of every 5th pupil on the register or every 20th would depend on the resources (time and money) available, the size of the school and whether parents were being consulted separately. If the school, however, only wished to consult parents with two or more children or families out of work, then these specific groups would form the research population.

As regards Munn and Drever's second point about 'the chances of one being selected independently of the other', it could at first sight seem to distort the sample if both parents in one household received a questionnaire while their neighbour had none. And yet, if these were the names which were randomly selected, they must go forward. The researcher is not allowed to depart from the principles, for in selecting a preferred group, e.g. 'those who understand' or 'those who are likely to give the kinds of answers I would like to hear', the sample would be biased and little reliable information could be gained from all the hard work!

Example

Research topic: A survey of local opinion to help plan a twice weekly activities afternoon to be held in the school hall.

Aim: Fund raising for school funds.

Research strategy: A questionnaire to be distributed to (? population) to find out:
1. whether they would be likely to participate in activity sessions on a regular basis;
2. what activities they would choose to have;
3. whether they would be prepared to pay, daily, weekly or monthly for the activity sessions.

Resources: The hall is available on three afternoons. The school canteen facilities could be used. If computing was a choice, three computers could be available. Table tennis, badminton, aerobics are all possibilities. These would be on a hired out system – who is to organise? Heating and lighting will have to be costed and the duplicating of the questionnaire and postage will have to be recouped from the fees.

Defining the research population, i.e. those who are to receive a questionnaire: Questions to be considered are:
• Every family in the neighbourhood? Where should the boundary be drawn?
• Households with elderly occupants? If not, what is the cut-off age?
• Households where both partners are known to work in the afternoons?
• Only parents with children in this school? What about local children at other schools?
• What about people with no children?
• Children (the session will begin at 1.30 pm). What age groups?
• Would creche facilities be a good thing? Extra cost?
• Families temporarily out of the district?
• Families with limited income?
• Only families who usually participate in community activities?

There are endless possibilities depending on the envisaged development. This list is simply to indicate the kind of pre-planning that is necessary if the correct population is to be identified. Thinking possibilities through and making informed choices allows the researchers to justify their choice, helps avert claims of bias if 'restricted groups' participate, or of 'wasted resources' if the 'wrong groups' are targeted.

Figure 4.9 shows the advantages and disadvantages of questionnaires.

Questionnaires	
Advantages	**Disadvantages**
Quick to administer	Time-consuming to design
Anonymous replies	Replies describe rather than explain
Many respones	Information could be superficial
No face-to-face interaction (no personal bias)	Unless coded, not easy to follow up interesting replies
Standardised questions	

Figure 4.9   The advantages and disadvantages of questionnaires

Interviews

The interview is a face-to-face interaction which allows the interviewer to ask carefully prepared questions and in addition to probe the respondents so that further information is obtained. The interviewer is hoping to be able to give explanations of why people's views are as they are, rather than knowing what a certain number of people said or did. At the interview, the interviewee has the opportunity to explain why the replies are as they are, and the interviewer, through noting non-verbal cues and factors such as the time between the question and the reply, can also record assessments of 'strength of feeling', or 'reluctance to reply'. The interviewee also has some freedom to expand on issues or to ask for clarification of a question or to put questions back in the interviewer's court.

At the start of the interview, pleasantries can help the interviewee to relax as can a brief prepared explanation (in user-friendly language) of what the interview is about. Assurances of confidentiality should be made early on, along with thanks to the interviewee for being prepared to take part. The interviewer must aim for a courteous, relaxed interaction. The interviewee must go away feeling that views and explanations have been valued and recorded accurately.

The setting
The setting for the interview is important. A degree of comfort and privacy is essential. This allows everyone to realise that the procedure is important and allows them to relax. If the interview is to be tape-recorded, then it goes without saying that an interviewer must be proficient in this skill. Nothing is more off-putting to the interviewee than to be halted

mid-stream because the machine is not recording properly, and to be asked to start again! It can also be very distracting if the interviewer's eyes are constantly checking levels of recording or whether there is enough tape left to record the whole interview. All the technicalities must be checked out before the interviewee arrives if the researcher is to have credibility.

Organisation
Times of interviews are arranged ahead of the day of action. If researchers can know the whereabouts of interviewees prior to the interview, they can be contacted if last-minute hitches prevent it taking place. The interviewee may be prepared to give a phone number for emergency only contact.

Time management
If interviews are sequentially arranged, it is better to leave a more than adequate time gap between each. This allows for late arrivals, loquacious participants and resetting the tape recorder. Interviewers will also wish to check that they have recorded all the vital information, including non-verbal cues which will not appear on the tape recording, and so time for immediate aide-mémoires should be allowed. Remember too that interviewing can be exhausting. Taking time to recharge both batteries and brains is a very necessary part of surviving to tell the tale.

Interview bias
While this research strategy is advantageous in gaining more qualitative information, the interviewer must be aware of all the sources of bias and try to reduce their influence. In any meeting or interaction, the two people immediately begin to make assumptions about each other and these can influence their responses. In an interview the respondent may be influenced by the interviewer's age, dress, manner and competence in handling the procedure as well as the choice of topic being studied and if that was not enough, the interviewer's own opinions may be deduced, either accurately or inaccurately, through voice intonation and non-verbal behaviour.

Aware of the difficulties however, researchers can take steps to reduce this bias. A useful first move can be for potential interviewers to practise the interview technique with friends, asking them to note behaviours which give clues as to the researcher's stance on the topic being studied. The next step is to try to reduce them – easier said than done, but essential if the interviewer is to be relaxed and confident and able to concentrate on the interaction.

Focus

The interview must stay on track, for it is very difficult to retrieve it once the topic is lost. Letting the respondent see that you are working from a schedule of questions can help. Perhaps at the start saying, 'I would like to ask you five questions about (the topic)' can both define the parameters of the interaction and suggest the amount of time to be spent on each. Preparing the questions in advance and staying with the prepared plan is an essential strategy. Researchers can then avoid having to think up questions as the interview proceeds, for this can communicate stress and perhaps even unintentionally pressurise the respondent into replying in a particular way.

Probing

The probes also need planning. 'Would you say a little more about that?' is less emotive than 'Gracious, tell me more' or 'Well, that's surprising...go on...!' Generally speaking, the interviewer should introduce the topic and then try to intervene as little as possible. A proficient interviewer can use silences or phatics (mmm...) or encouraging, rather than agreeing or disagreeing, facial expressions, i.e. different strategies which will help the interviewee to proceed. This is good practice, for the interview is not a chat or a discussion, it is a prepared opportunity to elicit the views of the interviewee and the explanations of why these views about the topic are held.

N.B. And so, interviewers must be able to encourage people who won't talk, quell others who won't stop and reroute others who go off at a tangent. An interview is not likely to be successful if the interviewer only prays for inspiration on the day!

Number of questions

As with the questionnaire, thought must be given to the number of questions, which will determine the length of the interview. It is a good idea to tell the interviewee in advance of the day that the interview is likely to last a certain time, say 15–20 minutes, so that pre-knowledge can prevent any irritation due to the interview taking too long or too short a time. While the complexity of the topic will determine the number of questions, the experience of the interviewer must also be taken into account. A short, to-the-point interview is likely to yield data which is vital and fresh, while a protracted interview can lack dynamism and become tedious.

Types of questions

All questions must be clear and unambiguous as in the questionnaire. While the interviewee docs have the opportunity to ask for clarification or explanation, reluctance to do this due to embarrassment or nervousness can mean that any misunderstanding can be passed over. If this happens and if, as a result, the interviewer does not fully understand the response, the whole quality of the interview is in jeopardy.

While the interviewer remains in control for nearly all of the time, the interviewee may wish to elaborate an issue or describe a related issue. The interviewer should allow space for this, asking for example, 'Are there questions you would like to ask me or any other points you would like to raise?' The skilled interviewer knows that listening can be as important as questioning, provided the talk is closely related to the topic at hand.

Statements

Another strategy is for the interviewer to read statements to the interviewee and ask for the degree of agreement or disagreement which the statement invokes. Ostensibly the statement 'comes from other people' and so reduces bias in the form of the interviewees' reluctance to disagree with the interviewers, if they are seen as the power figures in the interchange. Dillon's (1985) work claims that statements can be more provocative than questions which can inhibit the respondent. The example on p.89 of an Interview Schedule is based on statements. An interesting interview could combine different strategies.

Number of interviews

The time-consuming nature of the interview process usually means that only a small number of interviews can be held. The richness of the data with descriptions, explanations, justifications and additions from the interviewees' own experiences should compensate for the much smaller number of replies.

Anticipating the analysis

Analysing qualitative data is a very slow process involving transcribing tapes and interpreting the dialogue. Researchers should plan the number of interviews and the length of each in the knowledge that a lengthy procedure of analysis lies ahead.

Interview schedules

These schedules which the interviewer may hold during the interview (just like the market researcher in the street corner) can be helpful in:
- acting as an aide-mémoire for the researcher;
- letting the interviewee know that care has been taken in preparation;
- indicating that a number of questions have to be covered and that the responses will be carefully noted.

Example interview. Topic: Parents' evaluations of School Boards

Interviewer begins, 'I am trying to find out how different people who were elected to School Boards feel about the experience. I have a number of statements listed here. These were made by parents who served on School Boards at a number of different schools. It would be helpful to know whether you feel the same way about your experience or if you have a different view. There are no right or wrong answers, I am just hoping to get a true evaluation from different people to help the preparation of the next group of meetings.

Please say if you agree or disagree with these statements, or say if you are not sure. After that it would be helpful if you could tell me about your own experiences. (Figure 4.10 gives an example of an interview schedule.)

	Agrees	Disagrees	Don't Know	Other Response
1. The school has welcomed the formation of the School Board and has provided support and information to allow it to function properly.				
2. The composition of parents on the Board is not representative of the children in the school.				
3. The advice given by the Board has been acted upon.				
4. The head teacher and members of staff are the most powerful people in the group. Other members are influenced by their decisions to an unacceptable extent.				
5. The parents on the Board are really only concerned with what will affect their own children.				

Figure 4.10   Interview schedule: School Boards

Alternatively the researcher might prefer to ask the questions in a less formal way e.g. 'I wonder if you would like to tell me about being a member of the School Board?' In this situation the interviewee could well cover aspects not on the interview schedule, however, if the points 1–5 form the crux of the interview, the interviewer should anticipate the subsequent interaction and know how to (tactfully) elicit the required information. Remember that analysing replies to open questions can be difficult if the categories are obscure.

A table of the advantages and disadvantages of interviews can be found in Figure 4.11.

Interviews	
Advantages	**Disadvantages**
Researcher meets interviewee – personal exchange can help interpretation of meaning	Very time consuming, therefore fewer replies
Interesting answers can be followed through without delay	Levels of both procedural and personal bias can be high
Tape recording (with permission) can catch detail	Researcher may lead the interviewee – answers may be biased
Personal feedback obtained	Difficult to keep to the point
	The duo need time to relax and trust…

Figure 4.11 The advantages and disadvantages of interviews

CHAPTER 5

Analysing the data

The investigation has been carried out to provide evidence which will answer the research question and therefore explain why the changes have or have not achieved the postulated improvement in the teaching/learning situation. The evidence has been gathered using carefully constructed data gathering instruments, constructed, that is, to reduce bias and achieve reliability and validity.

The data is now ready for analysis. The raw data will have been amassed from different sources, different strategies and different research episodes (triangulation). The researchers must now study it all and pull meaning from the different records of evidence to identify constructs such as themes, incidence, patterns and trends. This is the critically important step in providing explanations of what occurred – rather than merely descriptions of what went on.

The key words or constructs in finding explanations are:
- themes   i.e. the consistent ideas which emerged;
- incidence*   i.e. how often something occurred or the number of questionnaire replies which said the same thing;
- patterns   i.e. the timing of the occurrences – whether they were single or in a cluster;
- trends   i.e. the frequency of the patterns.

It is only by comparing the data which emerged over several episodes that these can be identified and tallied and as a result the explanations and claims be justified.

*The question of how often an incident needs to happen before a claim is valid is a difficult one; certainly teachers would want to be convinced that the change was much more than a transitory blip or that there would be little likelihood of regression once the research was completed. This is one reason why sequential recordings over time make convincing reading.

Action researchers have to be careful to consider all the possible causes which are implicit in the data and not merely latch on to the most obvious as 'the' explanation. They must scrutinise the data for other factors which might have caused the change, e.g. could the improvement in behaviour have been due to the imminent parents' night as well as the innovation in the classroom? If no other impinging variables are found, then the first explanation stands. This critical analysis of the data allows claims to be made with confidence. No-one then can say, 'But what about…?', and uncover data which undermines, even disqualifies the claims that have been made.

Patton (1980) describes how this strategy of finding rival explanations should be carried out. He insists that researchers should not try to disprove alternative explanations (a negative plan) but instead, look for data to support them. In this positive mode, failure to find alternatives strengthens the original case.

A second point concerns operationalising the key concepts which are being recorded, i.e. spelling out exactly what they mean and thereby preventing misconceptions. If the hypothesis is, for example, that a certain input will help writing, the reader needs to know whether this means forming letters or writing stories. This may well have been explained alongside the data gathering instrument in the text, but it is best to remind the reader again in the findings chapter. Why? Because the reader may not have been able to read the whole report at one sitting and so needs to be reminded of the detail! Also, some readers begin by reading the synopsis and the findings, so all must be clear at every stage.

How should I record my findings?

Research within schools and particularly classrooms is not usually concerned with large numbers, and so sophisticated statistical analyses are not usually required. However, diagrams, tables and graphs can still usefully illustrate the findings. They make useful, concise reference points and break up solid text. They help readers who interpret visually more easily than through reading. In a small-scale investigation, however, they can be superfluous. There is no need, as one example, to construct a pie-chart to show that 50 per cent of a class of thirty children agreed with the issue in question. On the other hand, a graph showing a trend over time could be very informative and eye-catching even if small numbers were involved. The critical question is, 'What is the best way to report /display the data?'

In the findings chapter, the reader will expect to see the data collection instruments that were used. These can appear in the text or alternatively in the appendices, depending on their size. Extracts from each can illustrate the text, adding authenticity and interest to the reading, but the complete 'instrument' must be included in the appendix so that the reader can appreciate the extract in context. The researcher should also explain why the particular extract was selected. Was it representative of most others? Did it show a significantly different viewpoint? The reader will certainly want to know its relevance in the light of the whole study.

Data from case studies

If only a small number of children have been studied, then (just as in the context chapter where they were described in detail) their responses can be reported as individual case studies. The reader will 'know' the children by that time and will be very interested to find how each fared. But still the evidence must move beyond description; it is not enough to say 'John did this while Kate did that...' for the reader will simply ask, 'So what? What does this signify?' To answer, incidence, trends and patterns still have to be identified in the data and their meaning made clear. If the research question has included the phrase, 'to what extent' this provides a means of comparing each child's progress to the hypothesised improvement, or to the other children, and then contributing to cumulative evidence if this is appropriate. On the other hand, the researcher may wish to say that certain aspects towards improvement have been achieved by certain individuals while others need more practice.

Data from observation schedules

As the schedule was compiled, the researcher defined the categories that were to be observed and recorded, e.g. time on task; the number of social interactions children were engaged in; the various kinds of apparatus they chose to use; the teacher's own developing competence in settling the class. Each recording noted the incidence of these events and comparisons of sequential recordings should have thrown up patterns and trends. In the findings chapter, it can be helpful to insert one or two examples which provide evidence of the changes that occurred. Perhaps they could be reduced in size on a photocopier?

The implicit hypothesis within the research question anticipated that if such and such a change was made, there would be more of or less of the categories being observed. Studying the first schedule and the last would give evidence of any time change. Analysing each in relation to the contextual information, however, could give much more qualitative information about each day's events. Perhaps the recording was out of step one day because the child had a family crisis or was unwell? The benefit of action research in the classroom is that researchers have access to background information like this which adds meaning to the analysis.

Data from questionnaires

The questionnaire has provided a lot of information from a number of people. The questions were carefully conceptualised and piloted so that they were unambiguous and pertinent to the enquiry. There were a variety of types of question. These were to give interest and variety but also formulated with the analysis in mind. The lead-in questions, asked to put the respondents at their ease, may or may not form part of the critical analysis – if not, then these results can stay as tallies on the questionnaire completed to show final figures and placed in the appendix. The key questions with their answers need to be pulled into the text so that the reader can see the actual replies (numbers or text), and so evaluate the discussion and conclusions that follow.

The closed questions are easiest to analyse because the tallies immediately give incidence figures. These can be discussed in terms of what they mean for that context and then the totals, compared to other work, can show trends, e.g. 'In this study of 50 ten-year-olds, these middle children in the family were achieving... This compared favourably with —'s study which claimed...', or 'The twelve-year-olds in this study who identified playing computer games as their favourite hobby... This matched two of the three most recent research findings by "x" and "y" In contrast, "z" found...' This is factual reporting. The researcher has figures as evidence and in referring back to the literature can show how these findings compare to others, endorsing or refuting trends.

The answers to open question can be harder to analyse because the respondents have had some freedom to choose what they say. But careful reading and comparison allows categories of response to emerge. These can then be tabulated and discussed, just like the closed replies. However, there are likely to be explanations within these answers and this is what enlightens the analysis. Including extracts of one or two usual and unusual explanations in the text provides 'genuine' material for a lively discussion. Again they can be compared and contrasted with the themes and trends in the literature.

The answers to the closed questions just tell 'what' but give no reason why. There is loss of understanding (data degradation). The open questions have the facility to give more information and can provide a great deal of interest, even speculation. If the researcher wants or needs to know 'more', then these answers can be followed up by an interview session where probing can lead to more detailed explanations being obtained. But how does the researcher know the source of the interesting replies? This is only possible if the questionnaires have been coded – and then the question of anonymity/confidentiality and how its loss could increase bias has to be considered.

Students often ask if they should insert a blank questionnaire or a completed one in the appendix. The latter, completed in a child's writing, is a rich source of information and interest, quite apart from proving that the research actually happened! If the completed one is messy, obscuring the questions, the reader can refer to the one which has the answers tallied. The tallies themselves can be reported in a table in the text. This gives proof of the solidarity or disparity of replies.

N.B. Remember, as you study the responses to each question in turn and tally each kind of reply, that you are looking for trends rather than individual way-out replies. Having said that, it could be fascinating to read some unexpected thought-provoking replies. To clarify what was what, the researcher would be sure to say that these were one-offs and explain the reason for their inclusion.

Of course the thesis or report would be far too cumbersome if many questionnaires were included, so the researcher must select just a few, explain why they were chosen and keep the rest safe in case they are required by the examiners.

Data from audio recordings and interviews

Planned and practised audio recordings produce data which is free of procedural bias. As such they are 'true' recordings of interactions. The recordings do lack the meaning which is held in the non-verbals, although a little of this can be captured if silences and phatics are recorded alongside the verbals on the transcription of the interactions. These transcriptions are very time-consuming to analyse.

Again, as in analysing all data, the researchers must do more than repeat what was said. What does the conversation mean? What improvement or otherwise does it show? Is it throwing up any clues as to the child's difficulty or genius? How do the things being said lead to the conclusions and claims that are being made? And how do these compare/contrast with other studies in the literature?

Interviews have the added complication of procedural bias due to the interviewees' assumptions and the interviewer's skill or lack of skill in eliciting replies. However, the opportunity to probe and extract more meaning is there. The prepared interview schedule can be adapted to allow different responses to be tabulated and this can appear in the text so that the reader can have easy access to the raw data. However, this must be analysed to identify the incidence of pre-identified categories, the similarities in responses and what this means for the claims/explanations which follow.

N.B. Brief extracts in the text are helpful and revealing, but the full conversation should be in the appendix so that the reader can view it in context. Students need to check with their own awarding institutions how much has to be transcribed and retain the original tapes so that further listening is possible.

Data from video recordings

Video recordings, particularly helpful for showing movement patterns or social interactions, do provide a rich source of evidence, especially in making it possible to view and review specific incidents as often as is required. However, a full verbal explanation has to be made in the thesis or research report, because the reader may not be able to view the tape or even have the time/skill to make the necessary detailed observations. Photographs can be made from the film so that the thesis has stills of critical explanatory points, e.g. the lack of power in a child's arms shown in the way they are carried, but these are expensive to produce, and of course the author still has to explain why the picture is significant for the child's development and how this point relates to the input that is suggested or to the claims that are made. Certainly, video can give clear evidence of change over time and film may well be accepted as a data gathering instrument. But well in advance, be sure to check.

Summary points

- All data has to be reported and analysed.
- If extracts are reported in the text, the full documentation should go into the appendix to allow the reader to understand the extract in context.
- Summary reporting sheets allow tallies to be compiled and reported.
- Different 'answers' can be displayed in different ways, e.g. diagrams, tables, graphs (use graph paper), pie-charts or bar graphs. Choose logical and appropriate ones and explain what they mean if this is not obvious from the display.
- Stay with the identified categories. If these are not appropriate throughout the innovation, explain why.

- Consider the size of the claims you are making in relation to the amount of evidence you have. Be very wary of claiming generalisation unless steps to achieve this have been built into the research design.

N.B. Remember that explanations, not descriptions, are being sought. Remember that the research has tried to discover why...

CHAPTER 6

Writing a dissertation or thesis

The research report is a record of the process of your action research in school. It is subdivided into a number of chapters which sequentially house details of conceptualising and refining the research idea, justifying it in the context of the school and possibly in relation to the wider educational context, then planning, implementing and evaluating the action according to the principles of the action research method. The format provides a structure for the research 'story'.

Although writing up happens in retrospect, these notes, read at the start, can help you make decisions about the scope and extent of your investigation, for knowing what you have to report should help you plan what you have to do. And as you go through each stage, you can organise your notes, transcriptions and references into the appropriate section. In this way, some of the organisation is ongoing, reducing the final demand.

Each university will have written criteria to help you. There will be an allocated word length for the report and doing a rough subdivision right at the start can let you estimate how much detail you can afford for each section. Most universities allow a percentage over or under this total, but at the start it's best to aim for the 'right' length because this discipline can keep your writing focused and prevent you reporting interesting but irrelevant information.

Before going on to the actual composition of the report, a few hints and reminders could be helpful.

- Think of your reader as an educated lay person, i.e. someone who would understand 'usual' educational terminology but not the most difficult terms. Be sure to explain these. The reader needs to know that you understand, and are not just using words and phrases because they sound good, and yet the report must not be made cumbersome with unnecessary explanations. Aim for a balance.
- The methods chapter also needs clarification of terms. You must explain concepts like action research, bias and generalisation so that

the reader knows your stance and what principles guided your action plan. In a postgraduate thesis, the selection of action research as a method would need to be critically examined and justified at some length.

- It is also wise to envisage a reader who has not been involved in any of the discussions preceding the writing up. Sometimes students think, 'I won't need to explain that because my tutor knows...'. Remember, however, that it may not be your own tutor who marks your project, so if in doubt, explain.
- Write in the first person, e.g. 'I chose to do...' or 'my findings showed...'. This preserves the individual character of your research and your report; it keeps the text reader-friendly and helps the reader empathise with the events.
- Use the past tense throughout, even though at the start you are anticipating the action. 'At the start I did...I decided...I planned to ...I collected...' and so on. Be careful not to change tense as you write.
- It is often easier to write in the plural, i.e. talking about 'the children' rather than 'the child', because this avoids the he/she difficulty.
- Keep the purpose of the research clearly in mind as you write. You are carefully planning an action which will enhance your teaching and, through that, the learning experiences of your pupils. You are then monitoring the effects of that action in such a way that you can produce objective evidence of its effectiveness. In this way you can explain whether and in what ways the action has or has not helped your teaching improve. You would also wish to show if, and in what ways, the different pupils responded to the innovation.
- In similar vein, remember that you are only gathering information to answer your research question or test your hypothesis. The reader must be able to link the different parts of the thesis and read it as a clear and logical series of events which lead from the original idea through to the recommendations for further research which you make.
- Be sure to report what happened accurately. If something didn't work or if you got something wrong, then say so, and accompany this, if you can, with a suggested way of improving the action next time. Your reader will probably have been in school and will appreciate what rings true, and a totally smooth passage could just suggest that a superficial treatment had been given. Don't invent difficulties, but remember that discovering what is inappropriate for some children is a very useful research finding – provided of course, that the action was based on rational judgments in the first place!

- Whatever else, use the spell check, and after that reread the entire text slowly and carefully. Remember that the spell check cannot differentiate between e.g. practice as a noun and practise as a verb and other errors can slip through if they are real words, even though they are misused. It can be very irritating to have to read work that has been insufficiently checked. Furthermore, mistakes interrupt the reading and spoil the flow of the work. This can result in a poor grade.
- There is not one absolute way to write a report. You may wish to alter this plan to suit your investigation. If you do, be sure to cover all aspects. Check other research reports for alternative strategies and always discuss your plan with your tutor. Figure 6.1 gives the total picture in diagram form.

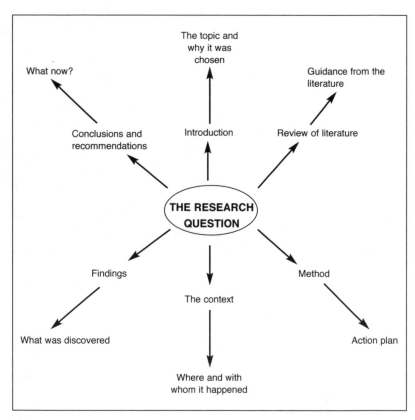

Figure 6.1   The whole picture

The format of the report

The cover will contain:
The title. Try to have a short title which captures the essence of the idea. For suggestions see pp.21 and 37.
The author's name (but see note below).
The tutor's name. Remember this is a formal document and give the tutor the correct title. Spelling the tutor's name correctly also shows care.
N.B. Some universities now prefer anonymous marking which means that the cover has no name, just a number. Stay with the rules!
Then the rest of your material will be organised as follows:

Pre-text		Acknowledgements
		Contents
		Synopsis
Text		Introduction
	Chapter 1	Review of Literature
	Chapter 2	Research Method
	Chapter 3	Research Context
	Chapter 4	Findings
	Chapter 5	Conclusions
		and recommendations for further research
Post text		Bibliography
		Appendices.

Pre-text

1. Acknowledgements
Here you have the opportunity to thank those who made a contribution to your investigation and to the compilation of the final report. This should be brief but apposite. You might thank your tutor for 'ongoing support', the teachers for 'making helpful suggestions and covering groups to allow data collection', the children for 'responding enthusiastically', the librarian for 'helping you find articles in journals', and the secretary for 'typing the report professionally'. Not all of these might apply, but a mention which is personalised like this can mean a lot to those who helped. It is a way of showing your appreciation.

2. The Contents page
This should be clearly set out and accurate.

3. The synopsis

The synopsis is a brief overview of the entire process. Complete the text and then pull back and identify one or two critically important points from each chapter. These have to provide the reader with a skeleton framework of events. Probably you would want to explain the purpose of your research, the main guidance from the literature, the research question, the action you took and the data gathering strategy which was used. You would then say what you found out and what would be the next logical step in any subsequent investigation. Write this last of all.

N.B. This is not the time to say obvious things like 'In the research methods chapter I show the methods I used.'

The text

1. The introduction

In the introduction you are setting the scene for your reader. You could usefully share the thinking and reflection which caused you to select your particular topic, and you would probably wish to explain the process of refining the original idea into a small-scale piece of action research and show how the literature influenced this process. Thereafter you could briefly describe the action you intended to take and say what teaching/learning enhancement you hoped would result.

2. The review of literature

In the review you show how your reading has informed and guided your action. In what ways has this information deepened your understanding? Have different authors made complementary and contrasting claims? Have you been able to identify common themes and show how the different research strategies others chose influenced their results? Have you selected quotations because they were phrased in the best possible way and have you ensured that you have explained any terminology which might not be obvious to the uninformed reader? Have you paraphrased other ideas but carefully acknowledged their original source, as of course you did with the quotations? You will remember that plagiarism must be avoided at all costs, and that even not intending to plagiarise is not likely to be accepted as an excuse.

Has your research idea derived from specific readings and have you shown how your research question has come from your reading? Is your plan a totally new idea or an extension of someone else's work or a repetition but in a very different context? Can you justify this?

Above all can you claim that you have read critically and analytically and that your review is much more than a series of quotes telling what other people have said? Your reader wants to know why you selected the key texts and how they influenced your decision making throughout the research.

Have you kept to one convention in acknowledging the work of others in the text? Do all the details correspond with those in the bibliography?

3. The research method

In this chapter you state your research question/hypothesis i.e. you clarify the central area of investigation. You may have written the research question at the end of the review to show how it emanates from the literature, but it is a good idea to state it again at the start of this chapter. This shows you are keeping it at the forefront of your thinking, and if the marker has a break in reading, then it is a helpful reminder.

The next task is to show how the emerging action has been planned according to the principles of action research. You aim to convince your reader that the data gathering strategies were carefully selected in the light of the participants, the context and what the purpose of the research was. You would explain what you did to reduce bias and the steps to try to achieve reliability. How were the research subjects chosen and what about the others? In what ways were they considered or was the research not important for them at all? It is best to explain all the detail if you want credit for the careful planning you have done.

It could be a good idea to justify your choice of strategy. Rather then say 'I decided to hold three interviews, on Monday morning,' a fuller explanation would show your understanding of the benefits and limitations of the different data collection strategies, e.g.

> At first I considered distributing a questionnaire to allow me to find what a large number of people thought, but on reflection I decided to hold just three interviews. Although this would not provide such a wide range of opinion, the issue was complex, and interviews would allow me to probe and discover...This would also overcome data degradation which can result from using questionnaires.

If you are using a case study approach you would disclaim generalisation at this point or say what steps you took to make it possible. And finally you would explain how you intended to analyse the data which you would collect.

4. The research context

In this chapter you describe the people and places and say what features of both influenced your choice of topic and perhaps how it was amended, e.g. how different issues became critical as the research was underway or perhaps how circumstances such as lack of resources influenced your action plan. Certainly you would take time to describe the children and why they were selected in some detail because this would allow the reader to visualise, appreciate and evaluate the sequences of action which you had planned, in the place where they were to happen.

5. The findings
The action has been taken and the important question(s)/hypothesis has been answered. The findings chapter tells what was discovered and therefore to what extent the envisaged teaching improvement facilitated the learning of the studied children. In this chapter you present the evidence of any claims that you make in clearly labelled diagrams or graphs or in descriptive writing. If you have few subjects, it is not necessary or even desirable to have statistical analyses, and certainly it is not necessary to produce a pie-chart to show 50 per cent. The reader wants a concise account of what was discovered. Diagrams and tables should clarify through providing evidence in another form, not simply be there for the sake of variety.

It is sometimes tricky to decide what evidence should go into the text and what into the appendices. The reader needs enough information in the text to save constantly referring to these appendices for figures or illustrative material; on the other hand the reading becomes fragmented if it is interrupted by too many figures and tables. Try to achieve a balance of critical information in the text with illustrative material in the appendices. 'Evidence' like children's drawings or stories is bulky. Can just one or two which clearly show evidence of the change be scaled down on the photocopier and therefore be inserted more readily into the text? One or two more can go into the appendix and there you can let your reader know that more drawings are available on request. Never part with any evidence – tapes or questionnaire or interview replies – until the thesis is safely marked. Transcriptions can go in the appendices with only short illustrative sections in the actual text. The source of these snippets has to be marked on the fuller transcriptions so that the reader can have easy access if this is necessary.

Sometimes students put blank questionnaires or observation schedules in the findings. This is not a good idea in my view. The reader needs proof that the research actually happened, and blanks don't convey that message. Even if the children have made their entries messy, a completed form in children's handwriting is a much more powerful piece of evidence, because it is authentic; you can also discuss how it was analysed or whether or not it was like other returns. All this as well as showing any difference in the child's competence!

6. Conclusions and recommendations for further research

This chapter asks 'What have you learned from all of this – and if you were to do it again what changes would you make or would you suggest that other researchers make?' Try to say more than 'Ah well, I'd take more time and have more children involved.' While this is often the case, you have an opportunity here to show that you have looked beyond the immediate benefits or frustrations and judged in the light of your experience what would be the most fortuitous thing to happen now. This is a chapter which looks back and then forward just like the first stage. Now of course you have a wealth of evidence and so can justify the suggestions for the best way to continue. The reader would be very interested in your evaluation of the research process and would want to know if the expectations of the research in terms of teaching and learning gain had been made.

N.B. Either in the findings chapter or in the conclusions or perhaps in both, you will look back at the advice or the different themes which emanated from the literature. How did your findings compare? What was it that caused them to be similar or perhaps completely different to what had gone before? If theorists offered different perspectives, how has your investigation informed that debate?

You will understand that each part of the write up has its own part to play in telling the research story. You have done a great deal of work and it is worth taking time to let others know the detail of what you found. This is important for generalisation.

Post text

1. Bibliography

In this section, accurate information about the literature used to inform the study has to be provided so that any reader can access the original source. One layout of books, journal and website articles and research reports can be seen in the bibliography of this text.

2. Appendices

This section houses tables, graphs, examples of schedules, fuller transcriptions, children's work – anything which illustrates the process of the research and yet was superfluous to the main text.

N.B. Different universities or other academic institutions may have different requirements. Always check!

The major aim of action research has been to develop meaningful practical wisdom in teachers. Somekh (1985) claims that it provides teachers with, '*A vision for learning, a high quality intellectual life...*' In view of all your hard work, I hope it has!

Bibliography

Abbs, P. (1985) *Art as a Way of Knowing*. Creative Education: University of Hull.

Argyle, M. (1960) *Bodily Communication*. London: Methuen.

Bell, J. (1993) *Doing your Research Project*. Buckingham: Open University Press.

Bradley, L. (1990) 'Rhyming connections in learning to read and spell', in Pumphrey, P.D. and Elliot, C.D. (eds) *Children's Difficulties in Reading, Spelling and Writing*. London: Falmer Press.

Brown, S. (1990) *Planning Small Scale Research*. Edinburgh: Scottish Council for Research in Education. (Spotlight 27.)

Bryant, I. (1996) 'Action research and reflective practice', in Scott, D. and Usher, R. (eds) *Understanding Educational Research*. London: Routledge.

Carr, W. and Kemmis, S. (1986) *Becoming Critical: Education, Knowledge and Action Research*. Lewes: Falmer.

Caseby, R. (1990) *Health Education Priorities for the Primary School Curriculum*: University of Exeter.

Child, D. (1986) *Psychology and the Teacher*, 4th edn. London: Holt Reinhart and Winston.

Dillon, J. (1985) 'Using questions to foil discussion', *Teacher and Teacher Education* **1**.

Ebbutt, D. (1985) 'Educational Action Reseach: Some general concerns and specific quibbles', in Burgess, R. (ed.) *Issues in Educational Research*. Lewes: Falmer.

Elliot, J. (1991) *Action Research for Educational Change*. Buckingham: Open University Press.

Elliot, J. (1993a) *Reconstructing Teacher Education*. London: Falmer Press.

Elliot, J. (1993b) 'Professional development in a land of choice and diversity; the future challenge for action research', in Bridges, D. and Keery, T. (eds) *Developing Teachers Professionally*. London: Routledge.

Gallahue, D.L. and Ozmun, J.C. (1995) *Understanding Motor Development*, 3rd edn. Madison WI: Brown and Benchmark.

Gomm, R. and Woods, P. (1993) *Educational Research in Action*. London: Paul Chapman.

Gow, L. and MacPherson, A. (1980) *Tell Them From Me*. Aberdeen: Aberdeen University Press.

Gurney, P. (1987) 'Self-esteem enhancement in children: A review of research findings', *Educational Research* **29** (2).

Harlen, W. and Schlapp, U. (1998) *Literature Reviews*. Edinburgh: Scottish Council for Research in Education. (Spotlight 71.)

Hopkins, D. (1994) *A Teacher's Guide to Classroom Research*, 2nd edn. Buckingham: Open University Press.

Hutt, C. (1979) 'Exploration and play' in Sutton-Smith, B. (ed.) *Play and Learning*. London: Garner Press.

Kirby, A. (1999) 'What should we call children's coordination problems? Dyspraxia or Developmental Coordination Disorder?' *Dyslexia Review*.

Lewis, I. and Munn, P. (1987) *So You Want to do Research? A guide for teachers on how to formulate research questions*. Edinburgh: Scottish Council for Research in Education.

Maccoby, E.E. (1990) *Social Development: Psychological Growth and the Parent–child Relationship*. New York: Harcourt Brace Jovanovich.

Macintyre, C. (1991) *Let's Find Why: A Practical Guide to Action Research in Schools*. Edinburgh: Moray House Publications.

Macintyre, C. (1998) 'Helping children with movement difficulties', *Education 3–13; The Professional Journal for Primary Education* **26** (1).

Macintyre, C. (2000) *Dyspraxia in the Early Years*. London: David Fulton Publishers.

McIntyre, D. (1993) 'Theory, theorisation and reflection in initial teacher education,' in Calderhead, J. and Gates, P. (eds) *Conceptualising Reflection in Teacher Development*. London: Falmer.

Munn, P. and Drever, E. (1990) *Using Questionnaires in Small Scale Research*. Edinburgh: Scottish Council for Research in Education.

Patton, M.Q. (1980) *Qualitative Evaluation Methods*. Beverly Hills CA: Sage

Rafferty, S. (1997) *Giving Children a Voice – What Next?* Edinburgh: Scottish Council for Research in Education.

Scott, D. and Usher, R. (1996) *Understanding Educational Research.* London: Routledge.

Somekh, B. (1995) 'The contribution of action research to development in social endeavours: A position paper on action research methodology', *British Educational Research Journal* **21** (3) June.

Stark, R. (1998) *Practitioner Research: The Purpose of Reviewing the Literature within an Inquiry.* Edinburgh: Scottish Council for Research in Education. (Spotlight 67.)

Verma, G.K. and Beard, R.M. (1981) *What is Educational Research? Perspectives on techniques of research.* Aldershot: Gower.

Index

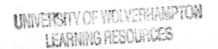